ADA5066

D1119138

APT
3/06

641.6565 Weinstein, Bruce,
WEI   1960-

       The ultimate peanut
       butter book.

C 2005

DATE			

SANTA CRUZ PUBLIC LIBRARY
Santa Cruz, California

BAKER & TAYLOR

OTHER BOOKS BY BRUCE WEINSTEIN AND MARK SCARBROUGH

The Ultimate Frozen Dessert Book
The Ultimate Chocolate Cookie Book
The Ultimate Muffin Book
The Ultimate Potato Book
The Ultimate Brownie Book
The Ultimate Shrimp Book
The Ultimate Candy Book
The Ultimate Party Drink Book
The Ultimate Ice Cream Book
Cooking for Two: 125 Recipes for Every Day and Those Special Nights

Savory and Sweet,
Breakfast to Dessert,
Hundreds of Ways
to Use America's
Favorite Spread

The Ultimate Peanut Butter Book

Bruce Weinstein and Mark Scarbrough

WILLIAM MORROW
An Imprint of HarperCollinsPublishers

THE ULTIMATE PEANUT BUTTER BOOK. Copyright © 2005 by Bruce Weinstein and Mark Scarbrough. All rights reserved. Printed in the United States of America. No part of this book may be used or reproduced in any manner whatsoever without written permission except in the case of brief quotations embodied in critical articles and reviews. For information address HarperCollins Publishers, 10 East 53rd Street, New York, NY 10022.

HarperCollins books may be purchased for educational, business, or sales promotional use. For information please write: Special Markets Department, HarperCollins Publishers, 10 East 53rd Street, New York, NY 10022.

FIRST EDITION

Designed by Renato Stanisic

Printed on acid-free paper

Library of Congress Cataloging-in-Publication Data has been filed for.

ISBN 0-06-056276-5

05   06   07   08   09   WBC/QW   10   9   8   7   6   5   4   3   2   1

ACKNOWLEDGMENTS

On the publishing end, much thanks to Harriet Bell, our publisher; Lucy Baker, our editor; Susan Ginsburg, our agent; Emily Saladino, her assistant; Carrie Bachman and Katherine Hanzalik, Harper's PR gurus; Ken Berger, terrific at special sales; Diane Aronson, a copy chief at Harper; Renato Stanisic, the designer; Beth Shepard, a PR whiz; Ann Cahn, our fabulous copy editor (who's now had a hand in every ultimate in one way or another, it seems); and Pat Adrian at Bookspan, a constant supporter—who first said, "Do a book on peanut butter."

On the professional end, our enduring thanks to Jason Laduca at Cohn & Wolfe for cases and cases of peanut butter; Brian Maynard at KitchenAid for his ongoing support; and Gretchen Holt and Stephanie Karlis at OXO GOOD GRIPS for a well-tooled kitchen.

But this book is ultimately dedicated to the kids who make us remember why we love peanut butter: the wonderful Gwen Kehrig-Darton (the only twelve-year-old who would go with us to modern dance), our over-the-top godson Max Kohlkins, his fabulous sister Allie Kohlkins, and the brilliant and beautiful Gilad Perlman-Greenberg.

CONTENTS

INTRODUCTION

Right about now, you may be thinking, who the heck needs a cookbook on peanut butter? Doesn't everyone know how to open a jar and spread some of the sticky stuff on bread?

If that's what you're wondering, then you, of all people, need this book. Peanut butter is far more than a spread. It's an American original, an invention up there with the likes of Model A's, apple pie, Mark Twain novels, ice cream cones, and Fanny Crosby hymns.

Still, most of us suffer from a lack of imagination when it comes to doing anything special with peanut butter. A cookie or two, and we're out of ideas. But it's high time we all picked up a wooden spoon and got to cooking with peanut butter. Frankly, it's hard to imagine an American kitchen without a jar. And since it's already got a spot on the kitchen shelf, why not give it a spot on the bookshelf, with a cookbook about making sauces, baking cakes, and blending up frozen drinks?

The history of peanut butter is a microcosm of U.S. history. It starts with European colonization and the slave trade, it gets a spark from two wars (Civil and World War II), it continues growing in popularity because of the can-do ingenuity of scientists like George Washington Carver, the make-a-buck machinations of small business owners like J. L. Rosefield, and the petty chicanery of schemers like Joseph Lambert, who may have dared to scam the mighty Kellogg brothers. (You'll find out more about all of them in *A Brief History of Peanut Butter*, pages 2–6.)

Finally, peanut butter gets ratcheted up the 1950s marketing pole because of the American fascination with doing things fast. But unlike a host of other fad conveniences, it's stood the test of time to become a twenty-first-century staple. (French sardines in mayonnaise or canned Harvard beets, anyone?)

What's more, peanut butter is the perfect fit with our series of nine other *Ultimate* cookbooks, a series devoted to America's favorite fun foods: ice cream, candy, party drinks, shrimp, potatoes, brownies, muffins, chocolate cookies, and frozen desserts. As you can see, we've gotten to be experts on indulgences, sweet to savory.

Like the other *Ultimate* books, this one includes recipes that can be customized to your own taste. We give you a solid base for, say, Peanut Butter Gingerbread or Thai Coconut Noodles, then we offer lots of ways to vary the dish by adding a splash of this or a smidgen of that, ways you can make the dish your own. For convenience' sake, the recipes are listed alphabetically within chapters, with the variations and customizations at the end of each recipe.

So stop that spreading and get to cooking—because almost everything's better with peanut butter.

A Brief History of Peanut Butter

2500 BCE The Incas grow the first peanut crops in Peru (peanut shells, archaeological digs). The Incas also grind peanuts with cocoa beans, probably for a ritual beverage, thereby starting the quasi-religious craze for peanut butter and chocolate.

mid-1500s Explorers and Jesuits bring peanuts back to Europe from the Americas. The plants do poorly in the Old World's chilly climate. They also meet with a PR disaster in the form for Bernabe Cobo, a priest who's been working in Peru. He claims the legumes are rank witchcraft. European cooks are easily dissuaded; Spanish and Portuguese traders, less so. To keep the goods flowing in the face of institutional objections, the traders take the new crop to Manila. Outside Cobo's reach, peanuts quickly spread to China and the East Indies (along with another New World wonder: chiles).

late 1600s To bolster their slave trade, Portuguese brokers transplant peanuts to sub-Saharan Africa as a cheap food source. The plants prove a natural in the hot climate and peanuts become an integral part of the region's cuisine.

mid-1700s African slaves take peanut plants on the horrific journey to North America.

Around 1800 The first known large-scale U.S. peanut crop is grown in South Carolina. Most peanuts are pressed for frying oil; some are ground as a stretcher for cocoa powder.

1801 A peanut farmer, Thomas Jefferson, is sworn in as the third president of the U.S.

1860 Confederate troops are given peanut rations to sustain them on their marches; for the first time in U.S. history, peanut consumption spikes noticeably.

1890 George A. Bayle Jr., a Saint Louis food manufacturer, is approached by a local physician who wants him to grind peanuts in one of his meat grinders so he can have a protein substitute for those with teeth so poor, they can no longer eat meat. The local physician isn't much of an entrepreneur, but Bayle begins selling peanut butter for 6¢ a pound.

1895 But Bayle isn't as quick as those consummate nineteenth-century entrepreneurs and health zealots, the Kellogg brothers of Battle Creek, Michigan, who apply for a patent to create a paste from nuts and legumes. On the application form, they claim peanuts create "a pasty adhesive substance that for convenience . . . is termed nut butter."

1896 The Kelloggs don't get the last word. Joseph Lambert, one of their employees and thus on the inside of a new fad, begins a small business selling hand-cranked nut grinders for home use. Three years later, his wife, Almeeta, joins the family business by writing *The Complete Guide to Nut Cookery*.

1903 In the South, Dr. George Washington Carver begins experimenting with peanut plants at Alabama's Tuskegee Institute. His initial work is to find crops that restore nitrogen to the soil.

1904 Back up north, Bayle, the Kelloggs, and the Lamberts are not to be outdone by Ambrose W. Straub who scoops them all by patenting a machine for making peanut butter. His problem? Like many inventors, he believes in the machine, not what it makes—so he goes into the grinder business, not the peanut butter business. Later that year, using one of those grinders, C. H. Sumner, a small-time food concessionaire, sets up a booth to sell peanut butter at the 1904 Universal Exhibition (the Saint Louis World's Fair, ground zero for all sorts of new wonders, including ice cream cones). He ends up selling $705.11 worth of the stuff, a veritable fortune at the time.

1905 A boll weevil plague almost wipes out southern agriculture. Dr. Carver convinces farmers to plant peanuts, not cotton. (By the end of the century, U.S. annual peanut production will reach 2 million metric tons.) Carver goes on to develop over three hundred uses for peanuts (including shoe polish and shaving cream), although he never patents any of his food ideas, claiming, "God gave them to me; how can I sell them to someone else?"

1908 With an abundance of peanuts now being grown in the South, Krema Products Company in Columbus, Ohio, begins selling bottled peanut butter at grocery stores. Krema's founder, Brenton Black, proudly claims he will never sell peanut butter "outside Ohio." It's an honest strategy at the time (peanut butter separates into a gritty paste and peanut oil, which goes rancid in days), but a bad marketing plan in the long run.

1922 J. L. Rosefield, a small business owner (Rosefield Packing Company in Alameda, California), develops a process for keeping the oil from separating from the butter and so makes modern, creamy peanut butter. He gives it a nostalgic twist and sells it as "hand-churned" peanut butter.

1923 Rosefield licenses his patented process to Swift & Company for its E. K. Pond Peanut Butter.

1928 E. K. Pond Peanut Butter isn't moving—the name, perhaps? So it's relaunched as Peter Pan Peanut Butter.

1933 Rosefield proves cantankerous when he realizes how much Swift & Company is making from his process, so he launches his own brand: Skippy Peanut Butter. With the coming of U.S. nationalism before World War II, Skippy is marketed in red, white, and blue rectangular tins.

1934 Rosefield begins trying to build brand extensions and so adds chopped peanuts to the mix, thereby creating the world's first crunchy peanut butter.

Around 1940 Separately, peanut butter and jelly are among the U.S. military rations. Many now theorize that GIs are the first to put the two together. In any event, the PB&J becomes a sensation in wartime America.

1955 The beginning of the modern peanut butter wars. BestFoods, Inc., buys the Rosefield Packing Company and becomes the maker of Skippy Peanut Butter. At about the same time, Procter & Gamble acquires W. T. Young Foods in Lexington, Kentucky, makers of Big Top Peanut Butter, a regional brand, and so throws its economic weight into the peanut-butter business.

1958 Procter & Gamble renames their peanut butter Jif. The plant in Lexington, Kentucky, soon becomes the world's largest producer of peanut butter, making over 250,000 jars a day.

1969 Cap'n Crunch's Peanut Butter Crunch cereal is introduced.

1974 March is declared National Peanut Month.

1977 A second peanut farmer, Jimmy Carter, is sworn in as the thirty-ninth president of the U.S.

1993 The world's largest PB&J is created in Peanut, Pennsylvania (40 feet long, 150 pounds of peanut butter, 50 pounds of jelly).

2002 The Oklahoma Peanut Commission and the Oklahoma Wheat Commission break the sandwich record in Oklahoma City with a sandwich weighing in at 900 pounds (with 350 pounds of peanut butter). It covers 60 square feet.

Peanut Butter Facts

- Peanuts are not nuts; they're legumes (that is, edible seeds enclosed in pods), closely related to peas.
- Peanut plants first flower aboveground, then bend over to dip their seedpods into the soil where the seeds come to maturity in their papery shells.
- Over half the U.S. peanut crop each year is churned into peanut butter.
- One acre of peanut plants will make about 30,000 PB&Js.
- It takes around 850 peanuts to make an 18-ounce jar of creamy peanut butter.
- An 18-ounce jar contains slightly less than 2 cups of peanut butter (about 2 tablespoons less, or 1⅞ cups).
- The USFDA requires that all peanut butter contain at least 90 percent peanuts. If it includes less, it must be labeled a peanut "spread."
- The average American schoolchild eats 1,500 PB&Js before graduating high school (about 125 a year, or 10½ a month).
- On average, a U.S. citizen eats about 3 pounds of peanut butter a year.
- Americans prefer creamy peanut butter to chunky by a 3 to 2 ratio.
- Women and kids overwhelmingly prefer creamy; men, chunky.
- People on the East Coast of the U.S. prefer creamy; people on the West Coast, chunky.
- Americans consume by far the most peanut butter of any citizenry in the world (around 800 million pounds a year), followed closely by the Canadians and Germans, with the English, Dutch, and Saudi Arabians rounding out the top contenders.

- Arachibutryophobia is the fear of getting peanut butter stuck on the roof of your mouth.

A Guide to Some Ingredients Used in the Recipes

Use this simple guide as a way to track down some of the unusual ingredients—or in the case of more commonplace ones, as a way to discover the rationale behind the recipes.

BLACK VINEGAR is a Chinese condiment made from pressed, fermented glutinous rice; it's sweetened and flavored with aromatics, usually star anise. It's available in most large supermarkets, almost all gourmet markets, and all Asian markets; or check out the Source Guide (pages 237–38) for mail-order suppliers. In every recipe, we also give you a formula to mix balsamic and Worcestershire sauce if you need to do some quick substituting.

BROWN SUGAR is made by processing granulated sugar with molasses. "Light" and "dark" simply indicate how much molasses is in the mix. By and large, we prefer dark brown sugar in these recipes because the deeper taste matches well with peanut butter.

Brown sugar clumps notoriously because the moisture evaporates over time, leaving the sticky crystals in nodules. Soften chumped brown sugar by placing it in a sealed, zip-closed bag and heating it in the microwave on high in 10-second increments until it's usable.

CHILI OIL is a fiery Asian condiment made from oil in which chiles have been steeped, thereby tinting it orange or red, but more importantly infusing it with the chemical inferno in the chiles' membranes and seeds. Chili oil should never be used as a cooking oil—rather, it's sprinkled on at the end to spike up the dish. By and large, Malaysian and Thai bottlings are hotter than Chinese ones. Because it goes rancid quickly after opening, store chili oil in the refrigerator.

CHILI PASTE is a fresh or fermented mixture of chiles, vegetables, and spices. Because there are hundreds of different kinds, experiment with various bottlings to discover which is right for your palette. We prefer Sambal Oelek, a fresh, chunky, banging-hot chili paste available in most markets and from mail-order suppliers (see the Source Guide, pages 237–38). When we're in the mood for something at the edge of tolerance, we go for Thai bottlings such as Sriracha Chili Sauce.

Most brands of CHOCOLATE are sold in several varieties: semisweet, bittersweet, and unsweetened. Basically, the names indicate the ratio of cocoa solids to sugar: semisweet has more sugar than bittersweet; both have much more than unsweetened. Milk chocolate adds milk solids to the mix; it's only called for in one recipe (Peanut Butter Cups, page 200).

Higher-end brands of chocolate often have a percentage marker on the label: 55, 66, or 71 percent, for example. This number represents the percentage of the mixture that is indeed cocoa solids. As a rule of thumb, consider anything in the 40s or 50s to be semisweet, anything in the 60s and 70s to be bittersweet. Unsweetened chocolate should be at least 95 percent.

Unless chips are called for, buy chocolate in baking bars. Store chocolate tightly wrapped in a cool, dark place.

There are two varieties of COCOA POWDER. 1) Dutched (or Dutch-style) has an added alkali that helps the cocoa solids dissolve in liquids, mellows their flavor somewhat, but also turns the powder darker. 2) Natural cocoa is missing the chemical additive and so is lighter in color but ironically darker in taste. A well-stocked pantry has both; we always indicate our preference, if any.

COCONUT MILK is made by soaking coconut meat in water and then pressing out the thick, viscous liquid. (There is no milk in coconut milk.) So-called "light coconut milk" is a subsequent pressing of the same coconut pieces with less fat being extracted a second (or even a third) time. By and large, we prefer light coconut milk in these recipes. We feel the reduced fat matches better with peanut butter. In no recipe do we call for cream of coconut, a sweetened concoction best for tiki drinks.

CONFECTIONERS' SUGAR (or "powdered sugar," or "icing sugar") is simply sugar ground finer than the standard granulated variety. Cornstarch is added so the pulverized crystals do not clump. A standard 1-pound box of confectioners' sugar contains 4 unsifted cups (or 4½ sifted cups).

Commercially-made CURRY POWDER is actually a mélange of up to twenty spices—no two brands are the same. Most bottled curry powder is yellow because it contains more turmeric by weight than any other spice. Madras curry powder is red from cayenne pepper—and much hotter. Look around your market and experiment with different bottlings, or see page 93 for a blend of dried spices that does the job from scratch.

We call for large EGGS—and we call for them at room temperature. Cold eggs can shock batter and can cause melted chocolate to seize (come apart into tacky little threads and a thin liquid). To get cold eggs quickly to room temperature, submerge them in a bowl of warm (never hot!) water for 5 minutes.

Always crack eggs on a flat surface. If you crack them on the rim of a bowl, you risk driving shell fragments and impurities into the white or yolk.

FISH SAUCE is the soy sauce of Southeast Asia. Made from fermented fish parts, salt, and aromatics, it has a pungent smell that mellows beautifully when heated or combined with other fats. Don't be put off: there is no substitute. But there are different varieties—nam pla (the very heady Thai bottlings), nuoc mam (the slightly sweeter Vietnamese bottlings), and fish gravy (the much milder Indonesian bottlings). You can buy fish sauce at almost all supermarkets these days, usually in the Asian aisle, although the selection at Asian grocers will be larger. Once opened, store fish sauce in the refrigerator.

A piece of fresh GINGER should have a sweet smell, a papery skin, and no wrinkled, mushy spots. Look for it in the produce aisle. Peel off the skin with a vegetable peeler or a knife, then either grate the ginger on a ginger board (available at cookware stores) or mince it with a knife. Jarred minced ginger has begun showing up in our markets, a convenience, for sure, and one you can store in your refrigerator for months on end. It can, however, ferment—check yours before using.

GINGER JUICE is simply the pressed juice from ginger. It's available in small bottles at most markets, usually alongside the condiments or sometimes in the Asian aisle. You can make your own by placing small chunks of peeled fresh ginger in a garlic press and then extracting as much juice as you need. Freezing ginger before you juice it breaks down the fibers and makes the job easier.

HOISIN SAUCE is a thick Asian condiment made from soybeans, garlic, sugar, spices, and vinegar. Chou hee sauce is a slightly stronger version of hoisin.

The quality of the HONEY you use will dramatically impact your final dish. Don't be afraid to experiment with exotic varieties like orange blossom, chestnut, oak, or our favorite, star thistle (see the Source Guide, page 237).

MARSHMALLOW FLUFF is an East Coast delight. West of the Mississippi, Fluff fades out and is mostly replaced by Marshmallow Crème, similar but slightly runnier. Either will work in these recipes; if you use Marshmallow Crème, you may need to add a little more confectioners' sugar to your icing or frosting.

We found that low-fat or even fat-free MILK actually works best when we're cooking and baking with peanut butter. Although whole milk is a baker's indulgence, peanut butter is already rich enough to make any dish an indulgence.

MIRIN is a sweetened rice wine, often used as a seasoning in Japanese dishes. It's sold in small bottles and can be stored in the pantry until it browns or develops a slimy cloud of participate material. In a pinch, you can substitute sweet sherry.

With PEANUT BUTTER, we're all familiar with the common distinction: creamy vs. crunchy. These recipes call for one or the other—crunchy is usually required for its texture. That said, almost any recipe can use either (except for quick breads and cakes where the extra weight of chopped peanuts can weigh down the batter). No recipe makes a distinction between "extra crunchy" and "crunchy" peanut butter.

However, there is one culinary distinction that does make a big difference: the one between standard peanut butter and so-called "natural" peanut butter. Both kinds are marked in the recipes—and the distinction should be observed. Standard peanut butter is made with peanuts, salt, and sweeteners (sugar for sure, but sometimes corn syrup and/or molasses), as well as hydrogenated oil which helps keep the peanut oil from separating in suspension. (If you've read "A Brief History of Peanut Butter" on pages 2–6, you know that the modern standard variety wasn't the standard through most of peanut butter's history.)

"Natural" peanut butter, by contrast, has no sugar and no hydrogenated fat, and so the oil often separates in the jar. Stir this oil back in for a creamier spread, or discard it for a less rich one. If you do stir it in, go slowly so as not to make a mess. Or a day or two in advance, turn the jar on its head so that the oil will percolate back through the peanut butter and soften it up. You'll still have to stir it up, but it will be much easier.

With the exception of only the first two recipes in this book, all call for jarred peanut butter. In the first two, you make your own peanut butter in a food processor. In fact, you can substitute these homemade concoctions for the creamy or crunchy standard peanut butter called for in any recipe.

Some high-end markets allow you to grind peanuts into peanut butter. Use this store-ground peanut butter as a substitute for the natural peanut butter in any recipe. One warning: the spread you make will lack any salt.

No-salt peanut butters of both standard and natural varieties and of both creamy and crunchy textures are also now in our markets. If you choose to use a no-salt version, you may want to adjust the salt of the final dish.

Finally, you can use "reduced fat" peanut butter for most savory and any drink recipe that calls for standard peanut butter. However, we do not recommend reduced-fat peanut butter for baking recipes since these have been calibrated with the requisite fat from the standard spread.

PEANUT OIL can be used as a base for any savory dish, and we prefer it for almost all stir-fries. Peanut oil can go rancid, thanks in large part to its relatively high content of polyunsaturated fats which are free to hook up with about anything that passes by in their environment. So store peanut oil in your refrigerator. It will cloud and may solidify, but you can return it to its liquid state by placing the bottle in a bowl of warm (not hot) water for 5 or 10 minutes. Always smell peanut oil to make sure it hasn't turned.

PRESERVED CHINESE VEGETABLES are a jarred Asian condiment made from mustard greens, cabbage, and/or radishes. Szechwan preserved vegetables, of course, are much spicier. The two can be used interchangeably, but the Szechwan version should be used sparingly until you get the hang of the heat. Look for either in the Asian aisle of gourmet markets or from Asian markets, or again, from mail-order suppliers (pages 237–38).

RICE VINEGAR is made from glutinous rice. It comes in two varieties: seasoned and regular (sometimes simply not marked as "seasoned"). The latter can be hard to track down except at Asian markets or through their suppliers. You can always substitute white wine vinegar or sherry vinegar for regular unseasoned rice vinegar, but the taste will be distinctly less sharp.

Seasoned rice vinegar is a Japanese product, usually used to make sushi rice (and sometimes labeled "sushi vinegar" in the U.S.). Better bottlings include a few aromatics in the batch, but the key ingredient for all brands is sugar. Substitute white wine vinegar plus ¼ teaspoon sugar per teaspoon used.

Although there are aged rice vinegars—usually tan to brown in color—we recommend only the clear products for these dishes.

Most of these recipes list SALT as optional. Since both standard and natural jarred peanut butter contain salt, always err on the side of caution. The only exceptions, of course, are if you grind your own peanut butter at the store or if you use bottlings marked "no salt" or "salt free." Then by all means add the salt to the recipe—unless, of course, your diet forbids it.

SESAME OIL is sold in two varieties: toasted and untoasted. We only call for the toasted kind; it has a deep, rich taste. Store it in the refrigerator and sniff it before using to make sure it hasn't gone rancid.

SHAO SHING (also bottled as Shaoxing, Shaohsing, or Huo Tiao) is a Chinese rice wine. In a pinch, substitute dry sherry.

SOY SAUCE actually comes in many varieties—from light to dark (not a reference to the sodium content but to how long it's aged after fermentation). Any will do, depending on your taste; but in these recipes, we advise you to steer clear of thick dark soy sauces and mushroom-based ones.

For health-conscious consumers, there are also low-sodium varieties. Frankly, we prefer these as a match to salty peanut butter in most of our dishes.

A few recipes call for SWEET SOY SAUCE: an Indonesian condiment that's thick and sweet. If you can't find it, make a sauce with 2 parts regular soy sauce and 1 part molasses, then use the amount of this mixture called for in the recipe.

TAMARIND PASTE is a thickener made from the ultrasour fruit of a shade tree native to Asia. Do not substitute tamarind syrup or pulp for the more concentrated, canned paste, available in East Indian markets, some Asian markets, gourmet stores, and from suppliers listed in the Source Guide (pages 237–38).

THAI CURRY PASTE comes in several varieties, all in various heat levels. Look for either green curry paste (with green chiles and aromatics) or red curry paste (with, obviously enough, red chiles). Some bottlings contain shrimp paste; all should be refrigerated once opened to preserve their freshness. For these recipes, do not use curry pastes made with clarified butter.

Although it's not the most popular type among U.S. consumers, UNSALTED BUTTER remains the baking standard and, thus, the only kind called for in these recipes. The sweet, creamy taste matches well with peanut butter; the lack of salt allows you to control the sodium content of the final dish.

The biggest myth in baking is the one about the butter's being at room temperature. When beaten, butter fat must be cooler than 68°F to trap air molecules (and thus build a batter's structure)—otherwise, butter simply flattens out into the smooth stuff we love to spread on bread. We recommend cutting refrigerator-cold butter into 1-tablespoon chunks and letting them sit at room temperature for 2 to 3 minutes before beating them.

UNSULPHURED MOLASSES has a clean, bright taste because it's made from sun-ripened sugarcane. Sulphured varieties are made from immature canes from which the juice is extracted with the help of a sulphurous gas. Obviously, we prefer the former.

Simply because it matches so well with peanut butter, we call for quite a bit of VANILLA in this book—some recipes ask for 1 or even 2 *tablespoons* of the stuff. Don't skimp on vanilla; buy the real thing. It's a baking indulgence that pays off in the final results.

The Classics

We had to start the book off with our ultimate versions of the great peanut butter sandwiches. Both are fully homemade: the bread, jam, peanut butter, and even the marshmallow cream! They're a lot of work—busy cooks may be tempted to bypass them—but once a year, break out the ultimate sandwiches and see how much applause a little work and a lot of peanut butter will bring.

THE ULTIMATE PB&J

Honey Oat Bread
Refrigerator Strawberry Jam
The Ultimate Creamy Peanut Butter

We're about to start turf wars. We think the ultimate PB&J is made with strawberry jam. Maybe it was a childhood in the late sixties when strawberry jam was starting to challenge grape jelly as top dog; maybe it's just that we like its texture with the Ultimate Creamy Peanut Butter. (More turf wars! You're free, of course, to use the Ultimate Crunchy Peanut Butter, page 22, and free to use any bottled jam or jelly you like.) This recipe makes a refrigerator jam, not processed or canned; simply store it in your refrigerator in sealed bottles or plastic containers for up to 2 weeks. What else do you need for the Ultimate PB&J? Fresh warm oat bread, of course.

MAKES 12 SANDWICHES

HONEY OAT BREAD

MAKES 2 LOAVES

2½ cups boiling water

1 cup rolled oats (do not use steel-cut or quick-cooking oats)

One ¼-ounce package active dry yeast

⅓ cup warm water, between 105°F and 115°F

2 tablespoons honey (see page 10)

2 tablespoons peanut oil, plus additional for greasing the bowl and pans

2 teaspoons salt

6 to 7 cups all-purpose flour

REFRIGERATOR STRAWBERRY JAM

MAKES ABOUT 1½ CUPS

3½ cups fresh hulled strawberries

2¼ cups sugar

¼ teaspoon salt

THE ULTIMATE CREAMY PEANUT BUTTER

MAKES ABOUT 1½ CUPS

2¼ cups dry-roasted salted peanuts (¾ pound)

1½ tablespoons unsalted butter

2 teaspoons light corn syrup

1. Pour the boiling water over the oats in a large bowl and set aside to soak until all the water has been absorbed and the mixture is lukewarm, stirring occasionally, about 1 hour.

2. About 5 minutes before you're ready to start making the bread, sprinkle the yeast over the warm water in a small bowl, stir gently, and set aside until frothy, about 3 minutes.

3. Stir the honey, oil, and 2 teaspoons salt into the softened oats, then stir in the dissolved yeast mixture.

4. *If you're using a stand mixer:* pour the yeast mixture into the attachable bowl, snap on the dough hook, and begin mixing the dough, adding the flour in ½-cup increments until a pliable but firm dough forms, one that's not sticky but is nonetheless stiffer than many white breads. You'll use more than 6 cups of flour, probably even 6¾ cups, but this will depend on the day's humidity and the glutens in the brand of flour you're using. Continue kneading at medium speed for 10 minutes, adding splashes of flour if the dough starts to stick or crawl up the hook. Don't use all the flour unless you need to—you simply want a smooth dough that's not tacky or gummy.

If you're working by hand: stir about 4 to 4½ cups of flour into the yeast mixture with a wooden spoon. Once the dough begins to form and becomes difficult to stir, turn it out onto a clean, floured work surface and begin kneading in more flour in small increments until a pliable, firm dough forms; continue dusting the work surface and your hands with ample flour to prevent sticking. Knead for 10 minutes, grinding the heel of one hand into the dough while pulling it with the fingers of the other, until the dough is smooth, somewhat elastic, but also a little stiff.

5. Grease a large bowl with peanut oil, gather the dough into a ball, place it in the bowl, and turn it over so that it's coated in the oil. Cover loosely with plastic wrap or a clean kitchen towel and set aside in a warm, draft-free place until doubled in bulk, about 1½ hours.

6. While the bread is rising, place a 2-cup heavy-duty resealable plastic container or a 1-pint glass canning jar and its ring lid in an empty dishwasher and run through a wash-and-dry cycle. If you don't have a dishwasher, use very hot, soapy water and rinse thoroughly. If you're working with a plastic container, it must be a heavy-duty one; flimsy containers will melt when the hot jam is spooned into them.

7. To make the strawberry jam, stir the strawberries, sugar, and salt in a medium saucepan over medium heat until the sugar dissolves and the strawberries begin to break down. Bring the mixture to a low simmer, then reduce the heat and cook slowly until thick and jamlike, about 20 minutes, perhaps longer if the day's humidity is high. If you're using a glass jar, spoon the jam into it while the jam and the jar are hot, then seal it with the lid and the ring; refrigerate the jar after 10 minutes. If you're using a plastic container, cool the jam for 10 minutes and then spoon it into the container, seal it, and immediately place it in the refrigerator.

8. Once the bread has doubled in bulk, remove the plastic wrap or the kitchen towel and gently but firmly plunge your fist into the dough, thereby deflating it without flattening it. Divide the dough in half and turn it out onto a clean, lightly floured work surface. Shape each loaf into logs about 8 inches long. Use peanut oil to grease two 5 × 9-inch loaf pans. Place the loaves in the pans, turn them over so they're coated with oil, cover loosely with plastic wrap or a kitchen towel, and set aside to rise until again doubled in bulk, about 1 hour.

9. Meanwhile, make the creamy peanut butter. Place the peanuts in a food processor fitted with the chopping blade; process until smooth—the heat and friction will release the peanut oil and the mixture will eventually convert from grainy to smooth. Add the butter and corn syrup; process until creamy. Set aside at room temperature until the bread is ready or spoon into a resealable plastic container and store at room temperature for 1 day or in the refrigerator for up to 2 weeks; stir well if any of the oil falls out of suspension.

10. Once the loaves have doubled in bulk, position the rack in the center of the oven and preheat the oven to 350°F. Bake the loaves in their pans until brown and somewhat hollow to the tap, about 40 minutes. Cool on a wire rack for 10 minutes, then turn the bread out of the pans and continue cooling for at least 10 more minutes before slicing, or until room temperature. Once the loaves have completely cooled, you can wrap them in plastic wrap and store them at room temperature for up to 3 days; or freeze them for up to 3 months, allowing them to thaw to room temperature on a wire rack before slicing.

11. To make the ultimate PB&J, use a serrated knife to slice the loaves into ¾-inch-thick slices (12 slices per loaf). Spread half the slices with 2 tablespoons homemade crunchy peanut butter; spread the other half with 2 tablespoons refrigerator strawberry jam. Place the bread slices together, peanut butter to jam, and chow down.

Want to take it over the top?

Before smearing on the peanut butter, spread the bread with a little softened unsalted butter.

Toast the slices before you spread them with the peanut butter and jam.

Layer apple slices, banana slices, or fried bacon strips onto the peanut butter before you close the sandwich.

Grill the sandwiches—just heat a grill, griddle, or sandwich maker and toast the sandwiches for no more than 1 minute on each side, just until the jam starts to melt.

Make hot sandwiches by melting 1 tablespoon unsalted butter in a large non-stick skillet set over medium heat. Slip one or two sandwiches into the pan; cook until brown, about 25 seconds; then flip and brown the other side. Repeat with more butter and sandwiches, as desired.

THE ULTIMATE PB&MARSHMALLOW CREAM SANDWICH

The Ultimate White Bread
Marshmallow Cream
The Ultimate Crunchy Peanut Butter

Marshmallow cream and crunchy peanut butter: now there's a combo right out of our childhoods. We brought these sandwiches to a New York City choir rehearsal one evening—they didn't do much for the singing, but they sure were a showstopper.

MAKES 12 SANDWICHES

THE ULTIMATE WHITE BREAD

MAKES 2 LOAVES

One ¼-ounce package active dry yeast
½ cup warm water, between 105°F and 115°F
3 cups whole milk
¼ cup sugar
2 tablespoons unsalted butter, plus additional for greasing the bowl and the
    pans
1 tablespoon salt
7 to 8 cups all-purpose flour

MARSHMALLOW CREAM

MAKES ABOUT 1½ CUPS

1 large egg white

⅓ cup plus 1 tablespoon light corn syrup

⅓ cup sugar

3 tablespoons water

1 tablespoon vanilla extract, or even a little more to taste

THE ULTIMATE CRUNCHY PEANUT BUTTER

MAKES ABOUT 1½ CUPS

2¼ cups dry-roasted salted peanuts (¾ pound)

1 tablespoon solid vegetable shortening

1½ teaspoons light corn syrup

1. Sprinkle the yeast over the warm water in a small bowl, stir gently, and then set aside until foamy, about 3 minutes. (If the mixture does not foam, start over—the yeast was bad or the water was too hot or too cold.)

2. Meanwhile, stir the milk, ¼ cup sugar, 2 tablespoons butter, and salt in a medium saucepan set over low heat until the sugar dissolves, the butter melts, and the mixture is just warm to the touch, certainly not hot, no more than 120°F (use a candy thermometer clipped to the inside of the bowl to be sure). Pour the milk mixture into the attachable bowl for a stand mixer or into a large mixing bowl, stir in the yeast mixture, and add 3 cups flour.

3. *If you're using a stand mixer:* attach the dough hook and begin mixing the dough at medium speed, adding flour in ½-cup increments until a soft and smooth dough forms, not sticky at all but quite pliable. Stop adding flour the moment the dough reaches this consistency and then continue kneading at medium speed for 10 minutes, adding small amounts of flour if the dough starts to crawl up the hook.

If you're working by hand: stir in about 1 to 2 more cups of flour with a wooden spoon just until a dough starts to cohere; then turn the dough onto a clean, well-floured work surface and begin kneading in more flour in ½-cup increments until a soft, smooth dough forms. Dust the work surface again with flour and continue kneading the dough for 10 minutes, digging into it with the heel of one hand while pulling it with the fingers of the other. Add more flour if the dough gets sticky, but do not add more than is absolutely necessary so that the bread does not turn out tough.

4. Place a small amount of butter on a piece of wax paper and grease a large bowl. Gather the dough into a ball, put it in the bowl, turn it over so that it's coated with butter, and cover the bowl loosely with plastic wrap or a clean kitchen towel. Set aside in a warm, draft-free place until doubled in bulk, about 1 hour.

5. Meanwhile, make the marshmallow cream by first beating the egg white in a second large bowl until foamy with an electric mixer at medium speed (if you're using a stand mixer, use the whisk attachment for this task). With the beaters running, slowly drizzle in 1 tablespoon of the corn syrup; continue beating until soft peaks form in the place where the turned-off beaters are lifted out of the mixture. Set aside.

6. Put the remaining ⅓ cup corn syrup, the ⅓ cup sugar, and the water in a medium saucepan and set it over medium heat, stirring with a wooden spoon until all the sugar dissolves. Clip a candy thermometer to the inside of the pan without its touching the bottom and continue cooking, without stirring, until the mixture reaches 248°F (often marked "firm-ball stage" on a candy thermometer; see Note). Remove the pan from the heat, remove the thermometer from the pan, and set aside.

7. Turn on the electric mixer at medium speed and beat the hot sugar syrup into the egg-white mixture in a slow, steady stream. Scrape down the sides of the bowl with a rubber spatula, then continue beating until thick, very white, creamy, but quite sticky, like the inside of warm, campfire marshmallows, about 5 minutes.

Beat in the vanilla. Remove the beaters or whisk attachment, scrape them down to get all the cream possible into the bowl, and set the mixture aside to cool for at least 10 minutes or until the bread has baked and cooled. To store, let the mixture cool to room temperature, then spoon it into a large 1-quart canning jar or a resealable plastic container and store in the refrigerator for up to 2 weeks.

8. When the bread dough has doubled in bulk, punch it down by gently pushing your fist into the mound, taking care to deflate it without flattening it. Cover again and set aside in the same warm, dry place to rise until again doubled in bulk, about 40 minutes.

9. Meanwhile, make the crunchy peanut butter by first placing 2 cups of the peanuts in a food processor fitted with the chopping blade. Process until the mixture flows smoothly around the bowl, then add the shortening and 1½ teaspoons corn syrup. Continue processing until smooth. Add the remaining ½ cup peanuts and pulse two or three times to chop lightly and combine. Set aside at room temperature until the bread is ready, or spoon into a resealable plastic container and store in the refrigerator for up to 1 week.

10. Once the bread has risen a second time, punch the loaf down again and then turn it out onto a clean, well-floured work surface. Divide the dough in half; shape and roll each half into a loaf about 8 inches long. Use a little butter on a piece of wax paper to grease two 5 × 9-inch loaf pans. Place each loaf in a pan, cover the pans loosely with plastic wrap or a clean kitchen towel, and set aside in a warm, draft-free place to rise until doubled in bulk, about 1 more hour.

11. After positioning the rack in the center of the oven, preheat the oven to 375°F.

12. Bake the loaves in the pans until brown and hollow when tapped, about 40 minutes. If you want, throw a crushed ice cube or two onto the oven's bottom when you first begin to bake the bread so that the steam will make a crunchier crust on the bread. Cool the loaves on a wire rack for 10 minutes, then turn them out of their pans and continue cooling for at least 10 minutes, or to room temperature. Once thoroughly cooled, the loaves can be wrapped in plastic wrap and stored at room temperature for up to 3 days, or they can be frozen for up to 3 months; thaw by unwrapping the loaves and letting them come to room temperature on a wire rack.

13. To make the sandwiches, slice the bread with a serrated knife into ¾-inch-thick slices (12 slices per loaf). Spread half the slices each with 2 tablespoons of the crunchy peanut butter; smear the other half of the bread slices each with 2 tablespoons of the marshmallow cream. Sandwich the slices together, peanut butter to marshmallow cream, and step out of the way of the impending stampede.

NOTE: *If you're boiling sugar syrup at high altitudes, you must adjust the temperature to account for the altered air pressure. Start by bringing some water to a boil in a saucepan, clip a candy thermometer to the inside of the pan without its touching the bottom, and measure the water's boiling point. Subtract this number from 212°F, then subtract this difference from any requisite candy-making temperature in the recipe. For example, if water boils at 206°F where you live, you need to deduct 6°F from the temperature to which the sugar syrup should be cooked.*

Want more than a regular ol' ultimate sandwich?

Spread a little butter or honey on each slice of bread before slathering on the peanut butter and marshmallow cream.

Spoon a little jam or jelly on top of the marshmallow cream before closing the sandwich.

Layer a thinly sliced banana on the sandwich before closing it.

Sprinkle on a few chocolate chips before closing it.

Breakfast

*No **wonder** people eat peanut butter on toast for breakfast—it's an easy hit of protein to start the day. Truth be told, there are lots more ways to get peanut butter into your favorite recipes: light peanut butter biscuits, peanut butter–stuffed French toast, and even the blowout, holiday-morning breakfast of peanut butter sticky buns. You may want to consider extending breakfast well into lunch!*

PEANUT BUTTER BISCUITS

Biscuits may be a southern religion, but we're not above enhancing them with peanut butter, one of the South's best products. Serve these with plenty of grape jelly on the side or try them with your own Refrigerator Strawberry Jam (page 17).

MAKES 8 BISCUITS

4 cups all-purpose flour, plus additional for dusting

1 tablespoon baking soda

¼ teaspoon salt, optional

½ cup creamy standard peanut butter

6 tablespoons solid vegetable shortening

1⅓ cups yogurt, preferably nonfat

1. Adjust the baking rack so it's in the center of the oven and preheat the oven to 400°F. Line a large baking sheet with a silicone baking mat or parchment paper; set aside.

2. Use a fork to mix the flour, baking soda, and salt, if using, in a large bowl until the baking soda is evenly distributed. Add the peanut butter and shortening; press through the tines of the fork or through those of a pastry cutter, pushing against the sides and bottom of the bowl to break up the peanut butter and shortening and mix it with the flour until the whole thing looks like coarse meal. Stir in the yogurt with the fork until a soft dough forms.

3. Dust a clean work surface with flour and turn the dough out onto it. Lightly flour the dough, then pat it with your hands until it's a circle about 12 inches round and ½ inch thick. Don't compress the dough; just press lightly with your fingers. Cut the circle into biscuits using a 2-inch-round cookie cutter, a 2-inch-round biscuit cutter, or a thick-rimmed, 2-inch-wide drinking glass.

4. Transfer the biscuits to the prepared baking sheet. You can gather the dough scraps together and press it again to make more biscuits, but the extra pressure and the extra flour on your work surface and in the dough will make the biscuits tougher. Bake until firm and golden, about 12 minutes. Cool on the baking sheet for 2 minutes, then serve at once.

Customize Them!

Add 1 teaspoon ground cinnamon, ½ teaspoon ground ginger, or ¼ teaspoon grated nutmeg with the baking soda.

Stir in ½ cup of any of the following with the yogurt: chopped dried apples, chopped dried apricots, chopped pitted dates, dried cranberries, dried currants, mini chocolate chips, or raisins.

Before they go in the oven, brush each biscuit with a mixture of 1 large egg white and 1 teaspoon water. You can also add 2 teaspoons sugar to this mixture.

Brush the unbaked biscuits with 2 tablespoons unsalted butter, melted and cooled, then sprinkle them with a mixture of 2 tablespoons sugar and 1½ teaspoons ground cinnamon.

PEANUT BUTTER COFFEE CAKE RING

Here's a yeast-raised, peanut butter–filled coffee cake you can even make ahead and freeze—just thaw it at room temperature on a wire rack for about 1 hour before serving, then pop it in a preheated 300°F oven for 10 minutes if you want to warm it up.

MAKES 1 COFFEE CAKE RING (ABOUT 12 SERVINGS)

⅓ cup warm milk (regular, low-fat, or nonfat), heated to about 115°F

¼ cup granulated sugar

One ¼-ounce package active dry yeast

3 large eggs, at room temperature

2 teaspoons vanilla extract

¼ teaspoon salt

¼ cup solid vegetable shortening, melted and cooled

4 tablespoons (½ stick) unsalted butter, melted and cooled

2½ to 3 cups all-purpose flour, plus additional for dusting

Nonstick spray

¾ cup crunchy standard peanut butter

¼ cup packed dark brown sugar

⅔ cup raisins

1. Pour the warm milk into a large bowl, stir in the sugar, then sprinkle the yeast over the top. Set aside until foamy, about 5 minutes. (If the yeast never foams, start over—the yeast was bad or the milk was too hot or cold.)

2. Use an electric mixer at medium speed to beat two of the eggs into the yeast mixture, then beat in the vanilla and salt until smooth. Beat in the shortening and butter until smooth.

3. *If you're using a stand mixer:* remove the beaters and attach the dough hook. Knead at low speed, adding more flour in ½-cup increments until a soft, pliable dough forms. Continue kneading for 5 minutes, adding small amounts of flour if the dough becomes sticky or starts to crawl up the hook. Because of the day's humidity, you may or may not use all 3 cups of flour.

If you're working by hand: stir about 2 cups of flour into the yeast mixture, maybe a little more, just until a dough starts to cohere. Dust a clean work surface with flour and turn the dough out onto it. Knead for 5 minutes, pressing the dough with the heel of one hand while stretching it away from you with the other. Add more flour sparingly should the dough become sticky; be sure to knead any extra flour fully into the dough.

4. Spray a large bowl with nonstick spray; gather the dough into a ball and place it in the bowl. Turn it over to coat it, then cover the bowl with a clean kitchen towel or plastic wrap. Set aside in a warm, dry place until doubled in bulk, about 1 hour.

5. Meanwhile, clean the beaters and make the filling. In a medium bowl, beat the peanut butter, dark brown sugar, raisins, and the remaining egg at medium speed until smooth. Set aside.

6. Once the dough has doubled in bulk, gently push your fist into it to deflate it, then turn it out onto a lightly floured work surface. Dust the dough and your rolling pin with flour, then roll the dough into a 15 × 20-inch rectangle with one of the longer sides facing you.

7. Spoon and spread the peanut butter filling onto the dough, leaving a 1-inch border on all sides. Starting with the long side closest to you, roll the dough into a tight log, taking care to keep the filling inside but still to make as compact a log as possible. Bring the ends of the log together to make a ring.

8. Line a large baking sheet with a silicone baking mat or parchment paper, then transfer the ring to it. Cover loosely with a clean kitchen towel or plastic wrap and set aside in a warm, dry place until doubled in bulk, about 1 hour. Meanwhile, position the rack in the center of the oven and preheat the oven to 350°.

9. Uncover the ring and use a sharp paring knife or a razor blade to make five equidistant slits across its top, each slit about 1 inch deep. Bake until lightly browned and the ring sounds hollow when tapped, about 35 minutes. Cool on the baking sheet for 5 minutes, then transfer to a wire rack to cool at least another 10 minutes before slicing. Serve warm—or cool completely, wrap tightly in plastic wrap, and freeze for up to 2 months.

Customize It!

You can replace the raisins with an equivalent amount of any of the following: chopped dried figs, cocoa nibs, dried cranberries, dried currants, or semisweet mini chocolate chips.

ORANGE GLAZE

Once the coffee cake ring has cooled, brush this easy glaze over the top right before you serve it.

> 2 tablespoons orange juice
> 2 teaspoons grated orange zest
> 2 teaspoons unsalted butter, melted and cooled
> 1 to 1¼ cups confectioners' sugar

Mix the orange juice, zest, and melted butter in a small bowl; stir in just enough confectioners' sugar so that a smooth, thick glaze forms. Drizzle over the coffee cake ring.

PEANUT BUTTER GRANOLA

Here's a new morning ritual: a healthy granola that's not loaded down with oil, but that's full of dried fruit, crunchy oats, healthy wheat germ, and (of course) peanut butter. Serve it with applesauce, milk, soy milk, yogurt, or cultured soy milk.

MAKES ABOUT 9 CUPS (OR ABOUT 9 SERVINGS)

4½ cups rolled oats (do not use steel-cut or quick-cooking oats)

1 cup wheat germ

1 cup unsalted sunflower seeds

½ cup powdered nonfat dry milk

2 teaspoons ground cinnamon

⅓ cup packed dark brown sugar

3 tablespoons apple juice

2 tablespoons unsulphured molasses (see Note)

2 tablespoons honey (see page 10)

¾ cup crunchy standard peanut butter

1 cup raisins

1. Position the racks in the top and bottom thirds of the oven; preheat the oven to 300°F. Mix the oats, wheat germ, sunflower seeds, powdered nonfat dry milk, and cinnamon in a large bowl; set aside.

2. Whisk the brown sugar, apple juice, molasses, and honey in a medium saucepan set over medium-low heat until the sugar dissolves. Whisk in the peanut butter until creamy. Pour this mixture over the dry ingredients and toss well with a wooden spoon—this takes quite a while because the mixture is stiff and there's no added oil in the liquid ingredients. Spread the granola onto 2 large, lipped nonstick baking sheets or 2 large baking sheets lined with silicone baking mats.

3. Bake for 20 minutes, stirring twice at 7-minute intervals; then reverse the sheets top to bottom and back to front and continue baking until dry, lightly browned, and very aromatic, about 25 more minutes, stirring often. Remove the sheets from the oven, place them on wire racks for 5 minutes, and then stir ½ cup raisins into the mixture on each sheet. Cool completely, about 2 hours. Transfer to a large or several small zip-closed plastic bags and store at room temperature for up to 1 month.

NOTE: *You can omit the molasses and increase the honey to ¼ cup, if you like.*

Customize It!

Substitute cranberry juice, orange juice, or white grape juice for the apple juice.

Add ¼ teaspoon grated nutmeg, ground allspice, and/or ground cloves with the cinnamon.

Stir ½ cup skinned, chopped hazelnuts or chopped walnuts into each tray after it's baked for 20 minutes.

Substitute an equivalent amount of chopped dried apples, chopped dried strawberries, dried blueberries, dried cranberries, or dried raspberries for the raisins.

PEANUT BUTTER JOHNNY CAKES

According to myth, Native Americans taught the American colonists how to make these cornmeal skillet cakes as a way to survive those first long winters. One thing's for certain: they didn't use peanut butter back then—but should have if they wanted to get through a winter's day.

MAKES 18 SMALL CAKES OR ABOUT 9 LARGE CAKES

1 cup all-purpose flour

1 cup yellow cornmeal

1 tablespoon sugar

2 teaspoons baking powder

½ teaspoon salt, optional

1 large egg, at room temperature

1¾ cups milk, preferably low-fat or nonfat

3 tablespoons creamy standard peanut butter

1 teaspoon vanilla extract

Nonstick spray

1. Mix the flour, cornmeal, sugar, baking powder, and salt, if using, in a large bowl until well combined; set aside.

2. In a blender, puree the egg, milk, peanut butter, and vanilla until smooth. (The recipe can be made up to this point up to 1 day in advance; cover both mixtures and store the liquid ingredients in the refrigerator until 30 minutes before you're ready to make the johnny cakes.)

3. Spray a large nonstick skillet or griddle with nonstick spray and heat it over medium-low heat.

4. Whisk the wet ingredients into the dry until fairly smooth; this will take a bit more whisking than standard pancake batter. Drop 2 tablespoons of the batter into the hot skillet or onto the griddle; continue making more cakes, as many as will fit. Cook until permanent bubbles dot the surfaces of the cakes, about 1½ minutes. Flip, then continue cooking until the bottom is brown, about 30 more seconds. Transfer the cakes to a platter and continue making more. (You may need to respray the skillet or griddle, but never spray directly into the flame or you could have a nasty fire on your hands.)

Customize Them!

Stir ⅓ cup fresh blueberries (small, wild blueberries work particularly well), mini chocolate chips, or raisins into the batter once you've whisked it smooth.

Substitute blue cornmeal for the yellow; add 2 teaspoons vegetable oil to the blender with the egg.

Serve Them Up!

Try them the old-fashioned way—with unsulphured molasses. Or try them with sweetened sour cream, sweetened whipped cream, fig preserves, raspberry preserves, or plenty of butter and maple syrup.

PEANUT BUTTER MUFFINS

We have another recipe for peanut butter muffins in *The Ultimate Muffin Book*, but there the point was to replicate the characteristic, fine-crumb texture of this favorite quick bread. Here, we're under no such bakerly compunctions, so we've developed a muffin where the point is truly the peanut butter, a dense, tender quick bread that's a great foil for honey or jam.

MAKES 12 LARGE MUFFINS

Nonstick spray or paper muffin cups

¾ cup plus 2 tablespoons all-purpose flour

⅓ cup graham cracker crumbs (see Notes)

1 tablespoon baking powder

¼ teaspoon salt, optional

¾ cup creamy standard peanut butter

⅔ cup sugar

4 tablespoons (½ stick) unsalted butter, melted and cooled

1 large egg plus 1 large egg white, at room temperature

2 teaspoons vanilla extract

½ cup plus 1 tablespoon milk, preferably low-fat or nonfat

1. Position the rack in the center of the oven and preheat the oven to 400°F. Lightly spray the 12 indentations of a standard muffin tin with nonstick spray, or line each indentation with a paper muffin cup (see Notes); set aside. Whisk the flour, graham cracker crumbs, baking powder, and salt, if using, in a medium bowl; set aside as well.

2. Beat the peanut butter, sugar, and butter in a large bowl with an electric mixer at medium speed until smooth, about 1 minute. Beat in the egg, then the egg white, and finally the vanilla until smooth. Scrape down the sides of the bowl with a rubber spatula and beat in the milk until creamy and light, about 1 minute.

3. Remove the beaters and stir in the prepared flour mixture with a wooden spoon or a rubber spatula, just until moistened. The batter may still be grainy but no white pockets of flour should be visible. Fill the muffin-tin indentations three-quarters full. Reserve any leftover batter for a second baking.

4. Bake until golden and a toothpick inserted into one of the muffins comes out dry, about 20 minutes. Cool the muffins in the tin on a wire rack for 5 minutes, then pop the muffins out of the tin and cool completely on the rack. They can be stored in an airtight container for up to 3 days. Or place them in a zip-closed plastic bag and freeze for up to 4 months; take them out frozen, tuck them in a backpack, and they'll be defrosted by midmorning, whether at work or on the hiking trail.

NOTES: *If you're not using purchased graham cracker crumbs, you can grind about 3 to 4 whole graham crackers in a food processor fitted with the chopping blade to make ⅓ cup of crumbs.*

Muffin tins don't come in standardized sizes. This recipe was developed for a tin in which each indentation holds about ⅓ cup batter. If yours holds more, increase the baking time by a few minutes; if less, decrease accordingly.

Customize Them!

Stir ⅔ cup dried cranberries, raisins, or semisweet chocolate chips in with the flour. Or add 1 teaspoon ground cinnamon with the vanilla.

EASY STREUSEL TOPPING

Here's an easy way to turn these muffins into the bakeshop streusel kind we all love.

> 4 tablespoons (½ stick) unsalted butter, melted and cooled
>
> 2 tablespoons packed dark brown sugar
>
> 2 tablespoons granulated sugar
>
> 3 to 4 tablespoons all-purpose flour or plain dry breadcrumbs

Mix the butter, brown sugar, and granulated sugar in a small bowl. Add the flour or breadcrumbs until crumbly but moist. Sprinkle evenly over the muffins before baking, about 2 teaspoons per muffin.

PEANUT BUTTER PANCAKES

A little peanut butter in the batter makes these tender pancakes hearty enough for a winter morning—or even for a summer one before a nice, long bike ride. If you want to serve the pancakes all at once, keep the prepared ones warm on a large baking sheet set in a preheated 170°F oven for up to 10 minutes while you make the rest.

MAKES ABOUT FOURTEEN 4-INCH PANCAKES

1¼ cups all-purpose flour

1 tablespoon baking powder

¼ teaspoon salt, optional

1 large egg, at room temperature

⅔ cup creamy standard peanut butter

3 tablespoons unsalted butter, melted and cooled

1¾ cups milk, preferably low-fat or nonfat

Nonstick spray

1. Whisk the flour, baking powder, and salt, if using, in a large bowl until the baking powder is evenly distributed; set aside.

2. Whisk the egg, peanut butter, and melted butter in a medium bowl until smooth. Whisk in the milk. (The recipe can be made ahead to this point—cover each bowl and store the dry ingredients at room temperature and the wet in the refrigerator for up to 12 hours; let the wet ingredients return to room temperature before proceeding.)

3. Spray a large nonstick skillet or griddle lightly with nonstick spray and heat it over medium-low heat. As it heats, stir the wet ingredients into the dry with a wooden spoon, just until the flour is moistened. The batter should still be a little lumpy.

4. Spoon a scant ¼ cup of the batter into the skillet to make one pancake. Add more batter to make more pancakes, as many as will fit. Cook just until the cakes have permanent bubble holes dotted across their surfaces. Flip with a nonstick-safe spatula; continue cooking until browned on the bottom, about 1 minute. Transfer to a platter or plates and continue making more pancakes.

Customize Them!

Whisk in 1 teaspoon ground cinnamon, apple pie spice mixture, or pumpkin pie spice mixture with the baking powder.

Stir ½ cup mini chocolate chips into the flour mixture before adding it to the wet ingredients.

Whisk in 2 teaspoons vanilla extract or 1 teaspoon maple extract with the milk.

PEANUT BUTTER SCONES

These scones are a tad lighter than the run-of-the-mill, bakeshop variety and thus a better match to the rich taste of peanut butter. If you like denser, chewier scones, omit the cake flour and use 2½ cups all-purpose flour. And be sure to save a few for tea or coffee in the middle of the afternoon.

MAKES 12 SCONES

1½ cups all-purpose flour, plus additional for dusting your work surface

1 cup cake flour

1½ teaspoons baking powder

½ teaspoon baking soda

¼ teaspoon salt, optional

6 tablespoons granulated sugar

⅓ cup packed light brown sugar

½ cup creamy standard peanut butter

3 tablespoons unsalted butter and 2 tablespoons unsalted butter, both melted and cooled in separate little bowls

1 cup heavy cream

1. Position the rack in the middle of the oven and preheat the oven to 425°F.

2. Whisk both flours, the baking powder, baking soda, and salt, if using, in a medium bowl. Use a pastry cutter or a fork to cut in 4 tablespoons (¼ cup) of the granulated sugar and all the brown sugar until uniform. Set aside.

3. Whisk the peanut butter and the 3 tablespoons melted butter in a large bowl until velvety. Whisk in the cream until smooth. Stir in the dry ingredients with a wooden spoon just until a soft dough forms; it will look a little grainy and rough. Knead a few times in the bowl until the dough holds together.

4. Lightly dust a clean, dry work surface with flour. Divide the dough in half and place each on the floured surface. Dust the pieces lightly with flour, then press or roll each into a 7-inch circle, about ½ inch thick. Brush each circle with half the 2 tablespoons melted butter; sprinkle 1 tablespoon of the remaining sugar over the top of each. Cut each circle into six, piece-of-pie, triangular wedges; place them all on a large nonstick baking sheet, spacing them about 2 inches apart.

5. Bake until lightly browned on the top and bottom, about 14 minutes. Cool on the baking sheet for 2 minutes, then transfer to a wire rack to cool completely. Store in an airtight container at room temperature for up to 2 days, or freeze between sheets of wax paper in an airtight container for up to 3 months; thaw on a wire rack at room temperature.

Customize Them!

Once the sugars have been added to the flour mixture, you can stir in ⅔ cup of any of the following or any combination of the following: chopped dried apples, chopped dried figs, chopped dried pears, chopped pitted dates, dried blueberries, dried cranberries, dried currants, raisins, or semisweet chocolate chips.

You can also whisk in 1 tablespoon vanilla extract, 1 teaspoon maple extract, or 1 teaspoon rum extract with the cream.

Make an easy vanilla glaze by combining ½ cup confectioners' sugar, 2 to 3 teaspoons milk, and 1 teaspoon vanilla extract in a small bowl; spread this on the scones once they're completely cool.

PEANUT BUTTER STICKY BUNS

Here's an over-the-top breakfast that's sure to be a hit any holiday when you serve it—or on any day you decide to turn into a holiday. To get the dough to rise, make sure the sour cream and eggs are at room temperature.

MAKES 16 STICKY BUNS

FOR THE STICKY BUNS

½ cup warm milk, preferably low-fat or nonfat, heated to 120°F–125°F

¼ cup granulated sugar

¼ cup packed dark brown sugar

One ¼-ounce package active dry yeast

½ cup sour cream (regular or low-fat but not nonfat), at room temperature

8 tablespoons (1 stick) unsalted butter, melted and cooled to lukewarm

2 large eggs, at room temperature

1 tablespoon ground cinnamon

½ teaspoon salt

3½ to 4½ cups all-purpose flour, or even more, plus additional for dusting

Nonstick spray

FOR THE FILLING

1½ cups crunchy standard peanut butter

1 cup raisins

½ cup packed dark brown sugar

1 teaspoon ground cinnamon

FOR THE TOPPING

⅓ cup packed light brown sugar

¼ cup honey (see page 10)

3 tablespoons unsalted butter, melted and cooled

1 cup chopped pecans

1. Pour the milk into a large bowl, whisk in the granulated sugar and ¼ cup dark brown sugar until dissolved, then sprinkle the yeast over the top. Set aside until foamy, about 5 minutes. Stir in the sour cream until smooth.

2. Beat in the melted butter, eggs, 1 tablespoon ground cinnamon, and salt with an electric mixer at medium speed until smooth and thick, about 1 minute. (If you're using a stand mixer, use the paddle beater for this step.) Switch the beaters' speed down to low and beat in 2 cups flour.

3. *If you're using a stand mixer:* scrape any dough off the paddle attachment, remove it, and attach the dough hook. Knead the dough at medium speed, adding more flour in ½-cup increments until a smooth, soft dough forms; continue kneading for 10 minutes, adding more flour if the dough sticks or climbs up the hook.

If you're working by hand: dust a clean work surface with flour and turn the dough out onto it, scraping the dough off the beaters and the side of the bowl. Knead, adding more flour in ½-cup increments, until the dough is no longer sticky. Continue kneading, pressing down with the heel of one hand while stretching the dough with your other hand until the dough is no longer sticky but soft and pliable, adding more flour to keep the dough pliable, but don't add too much or the sticky buns will be tough.

4. Spray a clean, large bowl with nonstick spray. Gather the dough into a ball and place it in the bowl, turning it over once to coat. Cover with a clean kitchen towel or plastic wrap, then set aside in a warm, dry place until doubled in bulk, about 2 hours.

5. Meanwhile, make the filling by mixing the peanut butter, raisins, ½ cup dark brown sugar, and 1 teaspoon cinnamon in a medium bowl until pastelike. Set aside.

6. Make the topping for the sticky buns. Mix the light brown sugar, honey, and melted and cooled butter in a second medium bowl; set aside.

7. Lightly spray a nonstick 9 × 13-inch baking pan with nonstick spray. Spread the topping mixture evenly in the pan, then sprinkle in the chopped pecans. (When the buns are baked and turned upside down, this will become the sticky topping everyone loves.)

8. Once the dough has doubled in volume, gently push your fist into it from the middle to deflate it, then divide it in half and turn out one-half onto a clean, lightly floured work surface.

9. Dust this half of the dough and your rolling pin with flour. Roll the dough into a 12 × 16-inch rectangle. Spread half the peanut butter and raisin filling over the surface of this dough. (If the filling is too hard, microwave it on high for 10 to 15 seconds to soften it a little, but don't get it hot.)

10. Roll the dough into a log, starting with one of the 16-inch sides. Slice it into 6 rolls, each about 2 inches thick. Place these in the prepared baking pan, spacing them 1 inch apart and offset from each other (one row down one long side of the pan, the next row spaced so that the buns lie to the side but also between the ones in the first row).

11. Repeat steps 9 and 10 with the second half of the dough, adding these rolls to the pan as indicated above. Cover the pan with plastic wrap and set aside in a warm, dry place until the rolls have doubled in bulk, about 1 hour. (Once the buns have doubled in bulk, you can refrigerate the pan for up to 12 hours before baking; return the pan to room temperature before proceeding.)

12. Position the rack in the center of the oven and preheat the oven to 375°F.

13. Remove the plastic wrap and bake the buns until golden and the filling bubbles in the cracks, about 30 minutes. When tapped, the buns should sound hollow. Cool in the pan for 10 minutes, then turn them out onto a large serving platter, letting the gooey topping drip over the buns. Serve at once or store at room temperature, tightly covered, for up to 2 days.

Customize Them!

Add 1 tablespoon vanilla extract with the eggs.

Substitute chopped dried strawberries or dried cranberries for the raisins.

Add ½ cup mini chocolate chips with the raisins.

Substitute chopped hazelnuts, walnuts, or unsalted peanuts for the pecans.

PEANUT BUTTER–STUFFED FRENCH TOAST

These are like fried peanut butter sandwiches—only with maple syrup. Double, triple, or quadruple the whole thing at will.

MAKES 4 PIECES STUFFED FRENCH TOAST (4 SERVINGS)

6 tablespoons creamy standard peanut butter

2 tablespoons cream cheese (regular, low-fat, or nonfat), at room temperature

Eight ½-inch-thick slices country-style white bread

6 large eggs

1 cup milk (regular, low-fat, or nonfat)

1 teaspoon vanilla extract

2 tablespoons unsalted butter, plus more if needed

Maple syrup for topping

1. Use a fork to mix the peanut butter and cream cheese together in a small bowl until smooth. Spread about ½ tablespoon of the mixture on each slice of bread, leaving a ½-inch border around the edge of each. Sandwich two pieces of bread together, thus making four peanut butter–cream cheese sandwiches; set them aside.

2. Whisk the eggs, milk, and vanilla in a 9-inch baking dish.

3. Melt 1 tablespoon of the butter in a large nonstick skillet set over medium heat, then dip two of the sandwiches in the egg mixture for a little less than 5 seconds per side. Let the excess drip off, then slip the two sandwiches into the pan. Cook until browned, about 1 minute, then flip and cook until the other side browns, about 1 more minute. Transfer to plates and repeat with the remaining two sandwiches. Serve at once with maple syrup.

Customize It!

Thinly slice 2 ripe bananas. In each sandwich, lay these slices on one side of the bread on top of the peanut butter mixture before closing the sandwich.

Sprinkle 1 tablespoon dried cranberries or raisins in each sandwich before closing it.

Spread 1 tablespoon jam or jelly in each sandwich before closing it (you'll need ¼ cup jam or jelly).

Dust the plates with confectioners' sugar before you serve them.

Don't just top these with maple syrup. What about blueberry, strawberry, or even coconut syrup? Or have you ever tried birch syrup? Maybe now's the time (see the Source Guide, page 237).

PEANUT BUTTER WAFFLES

For years, we've been partial to peanut butter on waffles—with maple syrup, of course. But then we discovered the joys of getting the peanut butter *inside* the waffles, which makes room for butter on top. This recipe is designed to make eight-inch waffles. If your iron makes larger ones, you'll need to use the required amount of batter, as indicated by the manufacturer's instructions. The good news? You can multiply this recipe by however many times you like.

MAKES SIX 8-INCH WAFFLES

1½ cups plus 2 tablespoons all-purpose flour

2 tablespoons sugar

1 tablespoon baking powder

¼ teaspoon salt, optional

2 large eggs, at room temperature

¼ cup peanut or vegetable oil

1¼ cups milk, preferably low-fat or nonfat

½ cup creamy standard peanut butter

1 teaspoon vanilla extract

Butter and maple syrup for topping

1. Whisk the flour, sugar, baking powder, and salt, if using, in a medium bowl; set aside.

2. Whisk the eggs and oil until uniform, then whisk in the milk, peanut butter, and vanilla. (The recipe can be made to here up to 12 hours ahead; cover both bowls and place the egg mixture in the refrigerator; let it return to room temperature before proceeding.)

3. Grease and heat the waffle iron according to the manufacturer's instructions.

4. Stir the flour mixture into the egg mixture with a wooden spoon just until moistened (the batter should still be a little lumpy—the trick to tender waffles is to get the flour incorporated without setting up any of its sticky glutens).

5. Pour a scant ½ cup of the batter into the heated waffle iron, close the lid, and cook according to the manufacturer's instructions. Serve at once with butter and maple syrup, or place the waffles on a large baking sheet in your oven, set it to 170°F, and continue making more, keeping the prepared ones warm in the oven in one layer on a large baking sheet.

Customize Them!

Substitute maple or rum extract for the vanilla.

Add ½ cup chopped pecans, mini chocolate chips, unsalted peanuts, or walnuts with the baking powder.

Breads

Baking with peanut butter is not as self-evident as it might seem. Since peanuts are legumes, they're not an immediate and easy fat substitute like some nut butters. Rather, the sugar and fat have to be calibrated to take into account the "drier" and "starchier" texture of peanut butter. So here's a set of moist, rich breads, all designed to take full advantage of that characteristic, peanut butter taste and texture. Most of these recipes are for quick breads—that is, breads that get their leavening from the frothy fizz of baking soda or baking powder—but there is one peanut butter yeast bread, perfect for the best grape jelly you can find.

PEANUT BUTTER APPLESAUCE BREAD

This sweet, relatively low-fat, easy, and nutritious quick bread is great for breakfast, an afternoon snack, or dessert.

MAKES 1 LOAF

1¼ cups all-purpose flour

½ teaspoon baking powder

½ teaspoon baking soda

½ teaspoon ground cinnamon

¼ teaspoon salt, optional

1 cup sugar

½ cup creamy standard peanut butter

¼ cup solid vegetable shortening, plus additional for the pan

1 large egg, at room temperature

1 cup unsweetened applesauce

2 teaspoons vanilla extract

1. Position the rack in the top third of the oven and preheat the oven to 350°F. Place a small dab of shortening on a piece of wax paper and use it to grease a 5 × 9-inch loaf pan, making sure you coat the corners and sides; set aside. Whisk the flour, baking powder, baking soda, cinnamon, and salt, if using, in a medium bowl until uniform; set aside.

2. Using an electric mixer at medium speed, beat the sugar, peanut butter, and shortening in a large bowl until light and creamy, about 2 minutes. Scrape down the sides of the bowl with a rubber spatula and beat in the egg until smooth. Beat in the applesauce and vanilla. Turn off the beaters, add the prepared flour mixture, and beat at a very low speed, just until moist if somewhat grainy (there should be no visible traces of white flour in the batter, but don't beat it so much that the glutens in the flour start to align and get stiff). Spoon into the prepared loaf pan, making sure it gets into the corners.

3. Bake until brown and a toothpick inserted into the middle of the loaf comes out with a few moist crumbs attached, about 55 minutes. Cool on a wire rack for 10 minutes, then turn the loaf out of the pan and continue cooling on the rack until room temperature, about 1 hour. Wrap the loaf in plastic wrap and store at room temperature for up to 4 days. Or freeze the wrapped loaf for up to 3 months; unseal and thaw at room temperature on a wire rack.

Customize It!

Add ¼ teaspoon grated nutmeg with the cinnamon.

Substitute 1 cup pureed canned unsweetened pears, pureed canned unsweetened apricots, or pureed canned pitted plums for the applesauce.

Stir in ⅔ cup chopped pecans, walnuts, or unsalted roasted peanuts with the dry ingredients.

Stir ½ cup semisweet chocolate chips with the dry ingredients.

Stir ¾ cup chopped dried apples, dried blueberries, dried cranberries, or raisins with the dry ingredients.

PEANUT BUTTER BANANA BREAD

Here's a quick bread that's moist and satisfying, thanks to all the peanut butter in the batter. It's also surprisingly low-fat, thanks to the ripe bananas. Consider it a peanut butter and banana sandwich, all baked together.

MAKES 1 LOAF

1¼ cups all-purpose flour, plus additional for the pan

1 teaspoon baking soda

½ teaspoon ground cinnamon

½ teaspoon baking powder

½ teaspoon salt, optional

1 cup crunchy standard peanut butter

⅔ cup sugar

2 tablespoons cool unsalted butter, cut into 2 pieces, plus additional for the pan

2 large eggs, at room temperature

2 large, ripe bananas, peeled and mashed (about 1 cup)

1 tablespoon vanilla extract

1. Position the rack in the center of the oven and preheat the oven to 350°F. Lightly butter and flour a 5 × 9-inch loaf pan; set aside. Whisk the flour, baking soda, cinnamon, baking powder, and salt, if using, in a medium bowl until evenly mixed; set aside.

2. Beat the peanut butter, sugar, and butter in a large bowl with an electric mixer at medium speed until light and creamy, about 1 minute. Beat in the eggs, one at a time, then beat in the mashed bananas and vanilla until smooth. Turn off the beaters, add the prepared flour mixture, and beat at a very low speed until a wet, sticky batter comes together. Spoon into the prepared loaf pan, gently getting the batter into the corners and smoothing the top.

3. Bake until golden brown, until a toothpick inserted in the bread comes out with a few moist crumbs attached, about 50 minutes. Cool on a wire rack for 10 minutes, then turn the bread out of the pan and continue cooling on the rack until room temperature. Wrap the loaf in plastic wrap and store at room temperature for up to 4 days. Or freeze the wrapped loaf for up to 3 months; unwrap and thaw on a wire rack at room temperature before serving.

Customize It!

Substitute 1 teaspoon pumpkin pie spice mix for the cinnamon.

Add ⅔ cup chopped pecans, chopped walnuts, chopped unsalted roasted peanuts, toasted pepitás (pumpkin seeds), or unsalted sunflower seeds with the baking powder.

Stir in ½ cup semisweet chocolate chips or cocoa nibs with the flour mixture.

Add 1 teaspoon maple extract or ½ teaspoon rum extract with the vanilla.

For a head-over-heels treat, toast slices of the bread and slather them with Refrigerator Strawberry Jam (see page 17 for a quick recipe).

PEANUT BUTTER CHOCOLATE TEA BREAD

These moist, chocolaty loaves are the perfect thing for a picnic, luncheon, weekend breakfast, or even a time-out in one of those ever-so-friendly games of bridge. Since there are two, there's enough to give to a friend—or to a partner who doesn't trump your ace.

MAKES 2 LOAVES

6 ounces semisweet chocolate, chopped

1⅓ cups all-purpose flour, plus additional for dusting the pans

1½ teaspoons baking powder

½ teaspoon salt, optional

¼ teaspoon ground cinnamon

12 tablespoons (1½ sticks) cool unsalted butter, cut into small chunks, plus additional for greasing the pans

1½ cups sugar

¾ cup creamy standard peanut butter

4 large eggs, at room temperature

⅓ cup milk (whole, low-fat, or nonfat)

2 teaspoons vanilla extract

1. Position the rack in the center of the oven and preheat the oven to 350°F. Lightly butter and flour two 4 × 9 × 2½-inch loaf pans (see Note); set aside.

2. Place the chocolate in the top half of a double boiler, then set it over the bottom part with about 1 inch of simmering water set over medium heat. If you don't have a double boiler, bring a similar amount of water to a simmer in a medium saucepan, then place the chocolate in a heat-safe bowl that fits snugly over the pan. Stir until half the chocolate has melted, taking care not to let any of the steam condense into the melting chocolate. Remove the top half of the double boiler or the bowl from the heat; continue stirring until all the chocolate has melted. Alternatively, melt the chocolate in a medium bowl in the microwave, heating on high in 15-second increments, stirring after each, until half the chocolate has melted; remove the bowl from the microwave oven and continue stirring until all the chocolate has melted. In any case, cool the melted chocolate for 5 minutes.

3. Whisk the flour, baking powder, salt, if using, and cinnamon in a medium bowl until uniform; set aside.

4. Beat the butter, sugar, and peanut butter in a large bowl with an electric mixer at medium speed until light and fluffy, about 2 minutes, scraping down the sides of the bowl as necessary. Beat in the eggs, one at a time, then beat in the milk until smooth. Scrape down the bowl and beat in the melted chocolate and vanilla. Turn off the beaters and remove them from the bowl, scraping any excess back into the batter. Stir in the prepared flour mixture with a wooden spoon, just until a smooth, moist batter forms. Spoon the batter evenly into the two prepared pans, smoothing it gently to the corners.

5. Bake until puffed and somewhat dry, until a toothpick inserted into the center of the loaves comes out with a few moist crumbs attached, about 45 minutes. Cool in the pans on a wire rack for 10 minutes, then turn the breads out onto the racks and continue cooling until room temperature. Wrap in plastic wrap to store at room temperature for up to 3 days. Or freeze the wrapped loaves for up to 3 months; unwrap and thaw at room temperature on a wire rack before serving.

NOTE: *These loaf pans are a little smaller than the standard 5 × 9-inch ones. We prefer them here because they don't hold as much batter, the loaves thus cook a little more quickly, and so the chocolate has a smaller chance of singing and turning bitter in the oven's heat. If you only have the standard, 5 × 9-inch pans, you can make one loaf of bread and then use the rest of the batter in greased muffin tins, or you can make two slightly squatter loaves in two 5 × 9 pans, but do watch them carefully so that they don't overbake.*

Customize It!

Stir in ¾ cup cocoa nibs or semisweet chocolate chips with the melted chocolate.

Stir in ⅔ cup chopped dried bananas, chopped dried strawberries, dried cranberries, dried currants, dried raspberries, or raisins with the melted chocolate.

PEANUT BUTTER GINGERBREAD

What's more inviting and warm than spicy gingerbread? Peanut butter actually heightens the tastes of the ginger and cinnamon, allowing them to play better against the tender richness.

MAKES NINE 3-INCH-SQUARE PIECES OF GINGERBREAD

1½ cups all-purpose flour, plus additional for the baking pan

1 tablespoon ground ginger

2 teaspoons ground cinnamon

2 teaspoons baking powder

½ teaspoon salt, optional

¼ teaspoon ground cloves

½ cup creamy standard peanut butter

⅓ cup solid vegetable shortening, plus additional for the baking pan

¾ cup unsulphured molasses

⅓ cup sugar

1 large egg, at room temperature

¾ cup plain yogurt, preferably low-fat or nonfat

1. Position the rack in the center of the oven and preheat the oven to 350°F. Place a small dab of shortening on a piece of wax paper and use it to grease the sides and bottom of a 9-inch-square pan. Put a small amount of flour in the pan, tap the pan so that it coats the bottom and sides, and knock out the excess.

2. Whisk the flour, ginger, cinnamon, baking powder, salt, if using, and cloves in a medium bowl until the spices and baking powder are evenly distributed in the mixture. Set aside.

3. Beat the peanut butter and shortening in a large bowl with an electric mixer at medium speed until smooth, about 1 minute. Add the molasses and sugar; continue beating until light and fluffy, about 1 more minute. Scrape down the sides of the bowl with a rubber spatula and beat in the egg, then the yogurt.

4. Turn off the beaters, pour in the flour mixture, and beat at a very low speed just until a wet if slightly grainy batter forms. Pour this mixture into the prepared pan, gently smoothing it to the corners.

5. Bake until a toothpick inserted into the center of the cake comes out with a few moist crumbs attached, about 35 minutes. Cool in the pan on a wire rack for 15 minutes, then turn the gingerbread upside down onto a cutting board to release it from the pan. Cut the cake into 9 squares. Serve at once, or return the squares to the wire rack to cool completely, about 20 more minutes. Wrap them individually in plastic wrap and store at room temperature for up to 3 days. Or freeze the wrapped squares for up to 2 months; unwrap and thaw to room temperature on a wire rack.

Customize It!

Add ⅔ cup of any of the following with the dry ingredients: chopped dried apples, chopped dried figs, chopped pecans, chopped unsalted roasted peanuts, chopped walnuts, cocoa nibs, dried cranberries, dried currants, or raisins.

PEANUT BUTTER QUICK BREAD

Here's a simple snack, perfect for any time of the day. It's best hot out of the oven, so make it just before friends arrive in the afternoon, or pop it in the oven just as you start that rented DVD in the evening.

MAKES 1 LOAF

Nonstick spray

2 cups all-purpose flour

1 tablespoon baking powder

½ teaspoon salt, optional

¾ cup creamy standard peanut butter

⅓ cup packed dark brown sugar

¼ cup granulated sugar

4 tablespoons (½ stick) unsalted butter, melted and cooled

2 large eggs, at room temperature

One 8-ounce can evaporated milk (regular, low-fat, or nonfat, see Notes)

2 teaspoons vanilla extract

1. Position the rack in the center of the oven; preheat the oven to 350°F. Lightly spray a 5 × 9 × 3-inch nonstick loaf pan with nonstick spray; set aside (see Notes). Whisk the flour, baking powder, and salt, if using, in a medium bowl; set aside.

2. Beat the peanut butter, brown sugar, and granulated sugar in a large bowl with an electric mixer at medium speed until pale brown and fairly smooth, about 2 minutes. Pour in the melted butter and continue beating until creamy. Beat in the eggs, one at a time, scraping down the sides of the bowl as necessary. With the beaters running, slowly pour in the evaporated milk, then beat in the vanilla. Turn off the beaters, add the flour mixture all at once, and beat at a very slow speed until a wet, fairly smooth batter forms (it may be grainy and even a little lumpy but there should be no white patches of flour visible). Pour into the prepared loaf pan.

3. Bake until golden and firm, until a toothpick inserted into the center of the loaf comes out with a few moist crumbs attached, about 45 minutes. Cool in the pan for 10 minutes, then turn the loaf out onto a wire rack and cool at least 10 minutes before slicing. Once completely cool, the loaf can be wrapped in plastic wrap and stored at room temperature for up to 3 days; it can also be frozen, wrapped in plastic wrap, for up to 3 months. Unwrap and let it come to room temperature on a wire rack, about 45 minutes.

NOTES: *Nonfat evaporated milk will make a slightly denser bread, with a crumb a bit more like fine cornbread.*
If you use a glass loaf pan, lower the oven's temperature to 325°F.

The Top Seven Things to Do with Peanut Butter Quick Bread

1. Cube it, spear it, and dip it into chocolate fondue.

2. Spread the slices with sweetened ricotta: 8 ounces regular or low-fat ricotta mixed with 2 tablespoons sugar and 2 teaspoons vanilla extract.

3. Make cinnamon toast by coating slices in a mixture of 2 tablespoons unsalted butter, melted and cooled, 2 tablespoons sugar, and 1 teaspoon ground cinnamon. Place them, buttered side up, under a preheated broiler until bubbling, about 1 minute.

4. Use the slices to make ice cream sandwiches. Smear your favorite flavor of softened ice cream on a slice, top with another slice, wrap individually in plastic wrap, and freeze until hardened.

5. Make a bread pudding out of it. In a large bowl, whisk 2 cups milk, 4 large eggs, ½ cup sugar, and 2 teaspoons vanilla extract until smooth. Cube the quick bread and stir these into the milk mixture, pour into a greased

9-inch-square pan and bake in a preheated 350°F oven until an inserted knife comes out clean, about 50 minutes.

6. Make a banana pudding by slicing the loaf and using these slices to line the bottom and sides of a 1½-quart casserole; cube the remainder of the slices. Make your favorite vanilla pudding (instant or otherwise) and stir in 2 sliced ripe bananas and the cubed quick bread. Pour into the pan and chill until set.

7. Make a peanut butter trifle. Cube the quick bread and douse it with a little sherry or brandy. Layer these slices in a large glass bowl (even a salad bowl will do) with canned peaches, fresh sliced strawberries, and vanilla pudding (regular or instant). Cover and refrigerate at least 4 hours to meld the flavors. Top with sweetened whipped cream before serving.

PEANUT BUTTER YEAST BREAD

And finally, one last peanut butter bread: an old-fashioned yeast bread with peanut butter in the dough. Despite the natural dryness of peanuts, peanut butter makes a surprisingly light bread, a great slice of toast any time of day.

MAKES TWO 9-INCH LOAVES

1½ cups milk (regular or low-fat, but not nonfat)

¾ cup creamy standard peanut butter

⅓ cup sugar

½ teaspoon salt

Two ¼-ounce packages dry active yeast

⅓ cup warm water (between 105°F and 115°F)

3 large eggs, at room temperature

2 tablespoons peanut or vegetable oil, plus additional for greasing the bowls

6 to 7 cups all-purpose flour

1. Heat the milk in a small saucepan over medium-low heat just until bubbles form around the inside rim of the pan. Do not boil, and do not allow the milk to form a skin.

2. Pour the milk in a large bowl and add the peanut butter, sugar, and salt. Use an electric mixer at low speed to beat until smooth. Set aside until the temperature is between 105°F and 115°F. (Do not continue with the recipe until the mixture reaches the right temperature.)

3. Sprinkle the yeast over the warm water in a small bowl, stir gently, and set aside to dissolve, about 1 minute.

4. Stir the yeast mixture into the peanut butter mixture. Beat in the eggs, one at a time, then beat in the oil until smooth. Beat in enough flour so that the mixture forms a wet but compact and cohesive dough.

5. *If you're using a stand mixer:* change to the dough hook and continue beating at low speed, adding flour in ½-cup increments, until you have a smooth, firm dough that's not sticky; then let the machine knead the dough for 10 more minutes. If the dough turns tacky or starts to climb up the hook, add a little flour, but be careful: too much flour and the bread can end up tough.

If you're working by hand: turn the dough out onto a well-floured work surface and begin kneading in the flour in ½-cup increments until a smooth, firm dough forms. Continue kneading until the dough is as smooth and soft as a baby's skin, pressing down with the heel of one hand and pulling the dough with the fingers of the other.

6. Grease a large bowl, add the dough to it, turn it over, and cover the bowl loosely with plastic wrap or a clean kitchen towel. Set aside in a warm, dry place until the dough doubles in bulk, 1½ to 2 hours. Meanwhile, grease two 9 × 5-inch loaf pans.

7. Uncover the bowl and gently but firmly plunge your fist into the dough, thereby punching it down without removing all the air. Divide the dough in half. Place one-half on a floured work surface and form into a 9-inch loaf. Place in one of the prepared loaf pans. Repeat with the other half of the dough. Cover each loaf pan loosely with plastic wrap or clean kitchen towels and set aside in a warm, dry place until doubled in bulk, about 2 hours.

8. Position the rack in the center of the oven and preheat the oven to 375°F.

9. Bake the bread until it is lightly browned and sounds hollow when tapped, about 30 minutes. Cool on a wire rack in the loaf pans for 10 minutes, then turn the loaves out of the pans and cool completely on the wire rack. Wrap the loaves in plastic wrap and store at room temperature for up to 3 days. Or freeze them for up to 3 months; unwrap and thaw at room temperature on a wire rack.

Want the best French toast?

Slice this bread and use it as the bread in Peanut Butter–Stuffed French Toast (page 47). Or forgo the peanut butter–cream cheese filling and simply dip these slices in the milk and egg mixture for regular French toast.

Sauces and Dressings

Anyone who's tried to make a good sauce knows how difficult it is to layer flavors and develop depth. Fortunately, peanut butter's done the job for you, providing a sweet, rich balance to spikier tastes like chiles and ginger. So here's a full set of sauces, mostly Asian—Vietnamese, Thai, Indonesian, and Szechwan. Most are served in splendid simplicity—over noodles—but we also offer lots of suggestions for other ways to enjoy these flavorful, intense sauces.

ANGEL HAIR PASTA WITH A THAI PEANUT SAUCE

We crafted this version of the classic Thai peanut sauce to be lower in fat and sugar than some traditional versions—a healthier way to eat, for sure, but just as tasty. The sauce is not pureed as it often is; we feel the chunky texture adds depth and stands up better to the heat. It's best over the tiny threadlike noodles known as angel pasta—more chewiness against the heat in each bite.

MAKES 4 SERVINGS

Nonstick spray

1 small onion, minced (about ⅓ cup)

1 garlic clove, minced

1½ tablespoons minced peeled fresh ginger

2 teaspoons chili paste (see page 7)

2 teaspoons packed dark brown sugar

¾ cup nonfat evaporated milk

½ cup chunky standard peanut butter

Juice of 1 lime (about 2 tablespoons)

8 ounces dried angel hair pasta or other thin pasta, or 12 ounces fresh pasta, cooked and drained according to the package's instructions

1. Spray a large nonstick skillet with nonstick spray and set the pan over medium heat. Add the onion, garlic, and ginger; sauté until fragrant and soft, about 1 minute. Stir in the chili paste and brown sugar; cook, stirring constantly, until very aromatic, about 15 seconds. Stir in the evaporated milk, peanut butter, and lime juice. Bring to a simmer, stirring constantly until the peanut butter dissolves into the sauce. Simmer for 10 seconds.

2. Pour the warm sauce over the noodles in a large bowl. Toss well and serve at once.

THAI COCONUT PEANUT SAUCE

Substitute ¾ cup coconut milk, preferably light coconut milk, for the nonfat evaporated milk.

Customize It!

With either the evaporated milk or coconut milk version of these sauces, you can also add 1 tablespoon fish sauce or 2 teaspoons tamarind paste (see pages 9, 12).

You can also substitute chunky natural peanut butter for a less sweet sauce.

You can puree either sauce in a blender or a food processor fitted with the chopping blade for a smoother, silkier texture.

You can also increase the chili paste to 1 tablespoon—but beware.

COLD PEANUT NOODLES

Anyone who's had Chinese takeout will recognize this noodle dish as our take on cold sesame noodles. In our version, peanut butter replaces the sesame paste, but we've retained the authentic sesame oil for its subtle taste. Adjust the heat according to your palate, or forgo the chili oil altogether for a sweet-and-sour version.

MAKES 4 SERVINGS

½ cup creamy standard peanut butter

6 tablespoons vegetable broth, preferably reduced-sodium broth

2 tablespoons toasted sesame oil (see page 12)

2 tablespoons soy sauce, preferably reduced-sodium soy sauce

1½ tablespoons rice vinegar (see page 11)

2 teaspoons Shao Shing (see page 12)

½ teaspoon sugar

½ teaspoon chili oil or a few dashes of Tabasco sauce

8 ounces dried spaghetti, or 12 ounces fresh spaghetti, cooked and drained
   according to the package instructions

2 scallions, thinly sliced

1. Whisk the peanut butter, broth, sesame oil, soy sauce, vinegar, Shao Shing, sugar, and chili oil or Tabasco sauce in a medium bowl until smooth. (The sauce can be made up to 3 days in advance.) Cover and refrigerate, then allow to come to room temperature before continuing with the recipe.

2. Toss the sauce with the noodles in a large bowl. Top with the scallions just before serving.

More Ideas

This piquant sauce is great over fresh egg noodles like fettuccine.

It's terrific over grilled or broiled chicken breasts, particularly if you serve them alongside a vinegary coleslaw.

You can thin out the sauce with more vegetable broth to make a rich dressing over a chunky vegetable salad of carrots, broccoli, and sugar snaps.

Serve the sauce as a dip for steamed or grilled shrimp, or set it out as a cocktail-hour appetizer dip with small rice crackers and celery ribs.

CUCUMBER NOODLES WITH A VINEGARY PEANUT SAUCE

We love cucumber noodles, long strips of cucumber made with a vegetable peeler. They're cool, refreshing, and a great match to this spiky sauce. They're also great for a summer picnic—just bring the sauce and cucumber noodles separately and toss them together right before you eat. For help with some of the more obscure ingredients here, check out pages 7–13.

MAKES 4 SERVINGS

6 tablespoons creamy standard peanut butter

2 tablespoons toasted sesame oil

2 tablespoons black vinegar, or 1 tablespoon balsamic vinegar and
   1 tablespoon Worcestershire sauce

1 tablespoon rice vinegar

1 tablespoon soy sauce, preferably reduced-sodium soy sauce

1½ teaspoons sugar

½ teaspoon chili oil

2 large cucumbers, peeled

1. Whisk the peanut butter, sesame oil, black vinegar, rice vinegar, soy sauce, sugar, and chili oil in a medium bowl until smooth. (The sauce can be made up to 3 days in advance; cover and refrigerate, then bring to room temperature before whisking again and proceeding with the recipe.)

2. To make the noodles, hold one peeled cucumber over a large bowl and run the peeler lightly over one side of it, thereby shaving off a long "noodle." Make a few more long strips, then rotate the cucumber a quarter turn or so and continue making "noodles," then do it from all sides until you get down to the seedy, pulpy middle—discard this and repeat with the other cucumber. (The cucumber noodles can be made up to 1 day in advance; cover and refrigerate until you're ready to make the dish.)

3. Place the cucumber noodles in a large serving bowl and toss with the sauce. Serve at once.

Want more things to do with this sauce?

Arrange the cucumber noodles on a platter, top with the Hacked Chicken (page 74), and spoon the sauce over the whole dish.

Use the sauce as a dip for fresh vegetables: cauliflower, broccoli, sugar snaps, or baby carrots.

Forgo the noodles and try the sauce over cooked spaghetti squash or as a dip for tortilla chips.

Thin the sauce out with some chicken or vegetable broth and use it as a dressing for a salad of chopped celery, chopped red onion, halved cherry tomatoes, and sliced almonds.

HACKED CHICKEN WITH A SZECHWAN PEANUT SAUCE

Here's a traditional Chinese dish that's perfect for a buffet or potluck. It should be served cold. The chicken and sauce can be stored separately in the refrigerator, then tossed together right before the dish is brought to the table. The sauce is actually a condiment for the chicken—the meat shouldn't be swimming in it. We prefer natural peanut butter here so that the sauce isn't quite so sweet.

MAKES 6 SERVINGS

¼ cup creamy natural peanut butter

¼ cup toasted sesame oil (see page 12)

2 tablespoons soy sauce, preferably reduced-sodium soy sauce

2 tablespoons black vinegar (see page 7), or 1 tablespoon balsamic vinegar
    and 1 tablespoon Worcestershire sauce

1 tablespoon sugar

1 tablespoon chili oil (see page 7), or less to taste

1 teaspoon grated orange zest

¼ teaspoon freshly ground black pepper

One 3-pound chicken, giblets and neck removed and discarded

One 4-inch piece fresh peeled ginger, cut into 4 chunks

6 scallions, cut into 2-inch chunks

4 garlic cloves

2 star anise

1. Whisk the peanut butter, sesame oil, soy sauce, black vinegar, sugar, chili oil, orange zest, and pepper in a medium bowl until smooth. Cover and refrigerate at least 4 hours or overnight.

2. Place the chicken, ginger, scallions, garlic, and star anise in a large saucepan or a large pot. Cover the chicken with cold water to a depth of at least 2 inches.

Place the pan over high heat, cover, and bring to a simmer. Reduce the heat and simmer until the meat is almost falling off the bones, about 40 minutes. Remove the pan from the heat, keep it covered, and let the pot stand at room temperature for 30 minutes.

3. Remove the chicken from the pot; discard all the aromatics (see Note). Remove the skin from the chicken and discard. Pull the meat off the bones and cut or shred it into uneven shards. Place the meat in a bowl, cover, and refrigerate until cold, at least 4 hours or overnight.

4. Mound the hacked chicken on a serving platter. Pour about half the sauce over the top and serve at once, passing the remaining sauce on the side for anyone who wants more.

NOTE: *The poaching liquid with the aromatics can be boiled down to make chicken broth, suitable for cooking, particularly in Asian dishes. Return the chicken bones to the pot, bring the mixture to a boil, then reduce the heat and simmer uncovered until reduced by half, about 40 minutes. Strain into glass jars and store in the refrigerator for up to 3 days; or let the broth cool somewhat, then strain into a sealable plastic container or several small ones and freeze until you're ready to use it, for up to 4 months.*

More Ideas

Once you mound the chicken on the platter and top it with sauce, sprinkle 2 tablespoons chopped toasted pecans, 2 tablespoons chopped roasted unsalted peanuts, or 1 tablespoon toasted sesame seeds over the dish.

Before placing it on the platter, toss the chicken with 3 chopped scallions, ½ cup minced celery, and/or ⅓ cup minced carrots.

This sauce is a fine spread for sandwiches and wraps, particularly those made with roast turkey. You can either use the sauce on its own or combine it with an equal amount of mayonnaise.

RICE NOODLES WITH A VIETNAMESE PEANUT SAUCE

Rice noodles are thin noodles made from rice starch. Once they're soaked in boiling water, they're ready to go. They make an easy addition to this classic Vietnamese sauce of peanut butter and coconut milk.

MAKES 4 SERVINGS

2 fresh serrano chiles, split open (seeds removed, if desired)

1 small shallot (both bulbs), quartered

1 small garlic clove

¼ cup packed fresh cilantro

½ cup plus 2 tablespoons creamy natural peanut butter

½ cup chicken broth, preferably reduced-sodium chicken broth

¼ cup coconut milk, preferably light coconut milk (see page 8)

2 tablespoons fish sauce (see page 9)

2 tablespoons packed light brown sugar

1 tablespoon tamarind paste (see page 12)

½ teaspoon freshly ground black pepper

16 ounces (1 pound) dried rice noodles or rice stick noodles, cooked and drained according to the package's instructions (see Note)

½ teaspoon ground cinnamon

1. Place the chiles, shallot, garlic, and cilantro in a large food processor fitted with the chopping blade; pulse until coarsely ground. Add the peanut butter, broth, coconut milk, fish sauce, brown sugar, tamarind paste, and black pepper. Process until smooth.

2. Toss the sauce with the noodles in a large bowl. Sprinkle the cinnamon over the top and serve at once.

NOTE: *Rice stick noodles are slightly wider versions of the traditional rice noodles; they are usually sold in dried bundles. Because the noodles do not expand when cooked, you should use more of them than you would for the same servings of Italian pasta.*

What to do with the sauce without the noodles?

Use it as a flavoring condiment for an easy stir-fry. After you've cooked some garlic and scallions in oil, add some shredded meat of your choice and some chopped broccoli or asparagus, stir-fry a minute or two more until the meat is cooked through, and stir in 2 tablespoons or more of the sauce. You can even add the soaked and drained rice noodles into the dish for the last few tosses to make a Southeast Asian–inspired noodle stir-fry.

SLAW WITH A PEANUT DRESSING

Here's our Indonesian interpretation of coleslaw, that American picnic favorite.

MAKES 6 SERVINGS

¼ cup creamy natural peanut butter

3 tablespoons lime juice

3 tablespoons toasted sesame oil (see page 12)

1 small shallot (both bulbs), minced

1 tablespoon sugar

1 tablespoon sweet soy sauce (see page 12); or 2 teaspoons soy sauce and
   1 teaspoon unsulphured molasses

1 teaspoon chili paste (see page 7—we prefer a Thai bottling with this slaw)

1 garlic clove, quartered

6 cups shredded Napa cabbage, shredded cabbage, or packaged coleslaw mix

1 large cucumber, peeled, then shredded through the large holes of a box
   grater

1. Place the peanut butter, lime juice, sesame oil, shallot, sugar, sweet soy sauce, chili paste, and garlic in a food processor fitted with the chopping blade or a mini food processor; blend until smooth, scraping down the sides of the bowl as necessary. (The dressing can be made up to 3 days in advance; cover and refrigerate, then allow to come to room temperature before whisking smooth and proceeding with the recipe.)

2. Place the cabbage and cucumber in a large bowl; toss with half the dressing, passing the remainder of the dressing on the side for those who would like more.

Customize It!

You can add any or several of the following to the vegetables before you dress them: 1 cup canned mandarin orange sections, 1 cup canned drained pineapple chunks, 1 cup shredded carrot, ½ cup chopped apple, ½ cup chopped celery, ½ cup chopped radishes, ½ cup raisins, ½ cup chopped red onion, ¼ cup chopped scallions, 2 tablespoons chopped roasted unsalted peanuts, or 2 tablespoons toasted sesame seeds.

SOBA NOODLES WITH GINGER PEANUT SAUCE

A Japanese favorite, soba noodles are made from buckwheat. They're available along with Asian noodles in most large supermarkets and all Asian grocery stores. This simple sauce is sour and very gingery, a nice match to the toothy noodles. If you want a sweeter sauce, use creamy standard peanut butter, not natural. The recipe only makes about ½ cup of sauce—less is more here, but you can always double or even triple the sauce recipe if you want leftovers.

MAKES 4 SERVINGS

¼ cup creamy natural peanut butter

3 tablespoons ginger juice (see page 9)

2 tablespoons soy sauce, preferably reduced-sodium soy sauce

2 tablespoons seasoned rice vinegar (see page 11)

5 dashes Tabasco sauce, or to taste

8 ounces dried soba noodles, cooked and drained according to the package's instructions

6 ounces snow peas, thinly sliced the long way and blanched (see Note)

1 red bell pepper, cored, seeded, and sliced as thinly as possible

1. Whisk the peanut butter, ginger juice, soy sauce, and rice vinegar in a small bowl until smooth, about like creamy salad dressing. Season with Tabasco sauce to taste. (You can make this sauce up to 1 week in advance; cover it tightly, store it in the refrigerator, and bring it to room temperature before whisking and serving.)

2. Place the cooked noodles, snow peas, and red bell pepper in a large bowl; pour in the peanut sauce and toss well. Serve at once.

NOTE: *The easiest way to blanch the snow peas is to toss them into the pot with the noodles during the last 10 to 15 seconds of cooking time. Drain and rinse them with the noodles under cool water.*

What to do with the sauce without the noodles?

Use this sauce as a condiment over steamed vegetables (particularly broccoli and asparagus).

Serve it on the side with roast chicken, pork, or salmon.

Use it as a stir-fry sauce—at the end of a stir-fry, stir in 1 to 2 tablespoons for flavor and garnish.

SPINACH NOODLES WITH PEANUT TOFU SAUCE

Tofu, which makes this Asian-inspired sauce so silky, comes in two basic varieties: firm and silken. The latter, called for here, is smoother and softer, better for sauces. Some popular brands, such as Mori-Nu, now sell "silken firm," a hybrid and equally good for this sauce.

MAKES 4 SERVINGS

¾ cup silken tofu

½ cup creamy standard peanut butter

3 tablespoons soy sauce, preferably reduced-sodium soy sauce

3 tablespoons red wine vinegar

1 tablespoon minced peeled fresh ginger

1 teaspoon sugar

8 ounces dried spinach noodles or 12 ounces fresh spinach noodles, cooked and drained according to the package's instructions

1. Place the tofu, peanut butter, soy sauce, red wine vinegar, ginger, and sugar in a food processor fitted with the chopping blade or in a wide-canister blender. Process or blend until smooth, scraping down the sides of the bowl as necessary. (The sauce can be made up to 3 days in advance; store it, covered, in the refrigerator but allow it to come to room temperature before proceeding with the recipe.)

2. Toss the noodles with the sauce in a large bowl. Serve at once.

What to do with the sauce without the noodles?

Make your own Asian-inspired burritos with a flour tortilla, some chopped radishes or radish sprouts, chopped tomatoes, Cucumber Noodles (page 72), and a little of this sauce.

Add lots of protein to grilled veggies by serving this sauce on the side.

Thin it out with a little vegetable or chicken broth and serve it as a dressing for a salad of sliced pears, Romaine lettuce, sliced red onion, and diced carrots.

Stir a tablespoon or two into any pot of beef stew right before you serve it to make a richer, creamier dish.

SZECHWAN SPICY NOODLES

This cooked sauce, a kind of Szechwan ragù, is often served as either a fiery starter or side dish. The ground pork adds texture and bite; the preserved Chinese vegetables lend an authentic taste. We find the sauce works best over thick, tubular noodles, such as the round egg noodles served with lo mein or even Japanese udon noodles.

MAKES 4 SERVINGS

2 tablespoons peanut oil

½ pound ground pork

4 scallions, thinly sliced

¼ cup chopped preserved Chinese vegetables (see page 11)

2 garlic cloves, minced

2 tablespoons minced peeled fresh ginger

2 tablespoons soy sauce, preferably reduced-sodium soy sauce

¾ cup chicken broth, preferably reduced-sodium broth

¼ cup creamy natural peanut butter

2 teaspoons chili paste (see page 7)

8 ounces dry lo-mein egg noodles or udon noodles, or 12 ounces fresh
   noodles, cooked and drained according to the package's instructions

1. Heat a medium saucepan over medium heat. Swirl in the peanut oil, then add the ground pork and cook, stirring frequently, until lightly browned, about 2 minutes. Add the scallions, preserved Chinese vegetables, garlic, ginger, and soy sauce; cook about 1 minute, stirring frequently. Whisk in the broth, peanut butter, and chili paste until smooth. Cook until simmering and slightly thickened, about 2 more minutes, stirring often. (The sauce can be made up to 2 days in advance; cover and refrigerate, then reheat in a medium saucepan with a little extra broth to thin it out, or in the microwave.)

2. Pour the sauce over the noodles in a large serving bowl, toss well, and serve at once.

Customize It!

Substitute an equivalent amount of ground beef for the pork. Do not use extra-lean ground beef or the sauce will be too dry.

You can also substitute ground turkey, but increase the oil to 3 tablespoons.

Or you can use textured soy protein, such as Yves' The Good Ground, Veggie Original Flavor; if you do, substitute vegetable broth for the chicken broth.

VEGETARIAN SUMMER ROLLS

This thick sauce is a condiment for fresh rice paper–wrapped rolls. They're not fried like egg rolls; instead, these Vietnamese wrappers are just soaked and softened, then filled with a fresh mix of veggies and sauce. The whole thing's light and easy, perfect for lunch or a snack on a hot afternoon. Look for rice paper wrappers in the Asian aisle of larger supermarkets or in all Asian markets.

MAKES 36 SUMMER ROLLS (ABOUT 12 APPETIZER OR 6 MAIN-COURSE SERVINGS)

½ cup creamy natural peanut butter

3 tablespoons toasted sesame oil (see page 12)

2 tablespoons black vinegar (see page 7), or 1 tablespoon balsamic vinegar
    and 1 tablespoon Worcestershire sauce

2 tablespoons soy sauce, preferably reduced-sodium soy sauce

2 teaspoons chili paste (see page 7)

1 teaspoon sugar

½ pound extra-firm tofu, finely chopped into small cubes

1 red bell pepper, cored, seeded, and shredded through the large hole of a
    box grater

1 cup shredded carrot

1 cup thinly sliced celery

36 rice paper wrappers

1. Use a whisk or a fork to mix the peanut butter, sesame oil, black vinegar, soy sauce, chili paste, and sugar in a large bowl until smooth. (The sauce can be made in advance up to 1 week ahead of time; cover and refrigerate until you're ready to use it.)

2. Toss the tofu, bell pepper, carrot, and celery into the sauce and stir well.

3. Fill a large shallow bowl, soup plate, or pie pan halfway with hot tap water. Gently submerge one rice paper wrapper in the water; keep it there just until it softens, about 20 seconds, but not too long or it will become fragile and tear when used. Lay the softened rice paper roll on a clean, dry work surface.

4. Place 2 tablespoons of the tofu and vegetable mixture in the center of the paper, making a small rectangle of filling. Fold the rice paper wrapper over the filling by taking the two edges of the circle nearest the short sides of the filling's rectangle and fold them up and over the filling. Then roll the wrapper closed, starting at the side of the circle nearest you and rolling away from you, thereby enclosing the filling inside the wrapper, like an egg roll. Set aside on a large serving platter, and cover with a sheet of plastic wrap and a barely damp kitchen towel over the plastic wrap.

5. Continue making the summer rolls, following the method in steps 2 and 3, until all the filling and wrappers are used. Once the water turns tepid, you'll need to pour it out and refill the dish with hot water. Serve at once or store in the refrigerator, tightly covered, for up to 2 hours.

Customize It!

Substitute 1 cup shredded radish, broccoli, garlic, or soybean sprouts for the carrot.

Substitute ½ pound precooked, peeled, deveined, and chopped medium cocktail shrimp (about 30 per pound) for the tofu.

Main Courses

In some ways, this chapter is the heart of the book. We Americans may have perfected the art of making cookies and cakes with peanut butter, but this spread actually finds its savory home in other parts of the world, particularly in Asia and Africa. Some of the dishes that follow are traditional— Pad Thai, Satay, Senegalese Peanut Stew—and some are, well, more whimsical: Peanut Butter Glazed Ham, for one. But they all use peanut butter in unexpected ways to showcase its ability to make a sauce, glaze, or thickener in no time at all, adding depth and flavor to many savory dishes.

AFRICAN GROUND NUT SOUP

Although there are many versions for this simple but hearty soup in central African cultures, our recipe has been adapted to accommodate western supermarkets. Ground nuts are a common nickname for peanuts, even in the American South (along with "goobers"). Here, they turn a vegetarian squash soup into a hearty warmer for a late winter night or an early spring evening.

MAKES 4 SERVINGS

2 tablespoons peanut oil

1 large onion, chopped

1 large red bell pepper, cored, seeded, and chopped

⅛ to ¼ teaspoon cayenne pepper or to taste

One 28-ounce can diced tomatoes, preferably no-salt diced tomatoes

1 medium kabocha, acorn, butternut, or blue hubbard squash, peeled, seeded, and cut into 1-inch cubes

2 cups reduced-sodium vegetable broth

¼ cup creamy natural peanut butter

8 kale leaves, stemmed and shredded

½ teaspoon salt, optional

¼ cup chopped unsalted roasted peanuts, for garnish

1. Heat a medium saucepan over medium-high heat. Swirl in the oil, then add the onion and bell pepper. Cook, stirring frequently, until softened, about 2 minutes.

2. Stir in the cayenne, cook for 5 seconds, then add the tomatoes, squash, and broth. Stir in the peanut butter until it dissolves. Cover, reduce the heat to low, and cook until the squash is soft, about 15 minutes, stirring once in a while.

3. Stir in the kale, cover again, and cook until the kale is tender and the squash starts to fall apart and thus thicken the soup, about 10 minutes. Season with salt, if desired, and serve at once, garnishing each bowl with 1 tablespoon chopped peanuts.

Customize It!

Add 1 tablespoon yellow curry powder, 2 teaspoons garam masala, 1 teaspoon ground cinnamon, or 2 bay leaves with the cayenne (discard the bay leaves before serving).

Increase the broth to 3 cups and add ½ pound cubed peeled yellow-flesh potatoes, such as Yukon golds, with the squash.

Omit the squash altogether and use 2 pounds sweet potatoes, peeled and cut into 1-inch cubes.

Add 1 pound chicken tenders with the kale or 1 pound boneless skinless chicken breasts cut into thin strips.

Add 1 pound medium shrimp (about 30 per pound), peeled and deveined (see page 101 for tips on how to do this), during the last 5 minutes of cooking.

CURRIED PEANUT SAUTÉ

Here's a satisfying, easy East Indian dish that'll hit the spot on a chilly evening—and cure that peanut butter craving, too! While the dish is made with bottled curry powder, you can substitute 1 tablespoon of one of the spice mélanges used in the Curried Peanut Stew (page 93). Serve the dish over wilted spinach or greens, or over an aromatic rice like jasmine, basmati, or Texmati.

MAKES 6 SERVINGS

2 tablespoons peanut oil

Six (4-ounce) boneless, skinless chicken breasts

1 medium onion, chopped

1 celery stalk, chopped (see Note)

2 tablespoons minced peeled fresh ginger

1 medium tart apple, such as Granny Smith or McIntosh, peeled, cored, and chopped

2 medium garlic cloves, minced

1⅓ cups chicken broth, preferably reduced-sodium broth

2 tablespoons creamy standard peanut butter

2 teaspoons yellow curry powder

½ teaspoon salt

1 bay leaf

1. Heat a large nonstick skillet or sauté pan over medium heat. Add the peanut oil, wait a few seconds, then add the chicken breasts. Brown one side, turn, then brown the other, for a total of about 6 minutes in the skillet. Transfer them to a plate, tent with foil, and set aside.

2. Add the onion, celery, and ginger; cook, stirring frequently, just until the onion softens a bit, about 2 minutes. Toss in the apple and garlic; continue cooking for

2 more minutes, stirring often. Meanwhile, whisk the broth and peanut butter in a small bowl until smooth; set aside.

3. Sprinkle the curry powder and salt over the vegetables, stir well, and tuck in the bay leaf. Pour the broth mixture over the vegetables and bring the mixture to a simmer, using a wooden spoon to scrape up any browned bits on the bottom of the pan.

4. Return the chicken breasts to the pan, coating them in the sauce. Cover the pan, reduce the heat, and simmer slowly until the breasts are cooked through, about 5 minutes. Discard the bay leaf and serve at once.

Customize It!

Substitute pork chops for the chicken breasts. Use thick-cut pork chops and a wide sauté pan. Increase the broth to 2 cups.

Substitute about 1½ pounds lean pork sausage or textured soy protein sausage for the chicken. If you're using soy sausage, do not brown it first in the pan—simply add it to the pan in step 4.

Substitute 1½ pounds medium shrimp (about 30 per pound), peeled and deveined for the chicken breasts (see page 101 for tips on dealing with shrimp). Omit cooking them in step 1; simply add them in step 4 when you would have returned the chicken to the pan.

CURRIED PEANUT STEW

This stew is made with a genuine curry—that is, a spice mélange you build yourself. The result is a deep, rich taste without a lot of fuss or time.

MAKES 4 SERVINGS

2 tablespoons peanut oil

8 skinless chicken thighs (about 3 pounds)

2 medium onions, roughly chopped

2 garlic cloves, minced

1½ teaspoons ground coriander

1 teaspoon dry mustard

1 teaspoon ground cinnamon

1 teaspoon ground cumin

1 teaspoon ground ginger

1 teaspoon turmeric

½ teaspoon freshly ground black pepper

1 cup reduced-sodium tomato sauce

½ cup creamy natural peanut butter

1½ cups vegetable broth

1 tablespoon apple cider vinegar

½ teaspoon salt, optional

2 cups cooked white rice

1. Heat a large, deep saucepan over medium heat. Pour in the oil, wait a second or two, then add the chicken thighs—in batches, if necessary. Brown them on both sides, about 2 minutes per side; transfer them to a plate and set aside.

2. Toss the onions into the pan and cook, stirring often, until somewhat softened, about 2 minutes. Add the garlic and cook for 15 seconds, then sprinkle in the ground coriander, dry mustard, cinnamon, cumin, ginger, turmeric, and pepper. Cook until aromatic, about 20 seconds.

3. Pour in the tomato sauce, scraping up any browned bits on the bottom of the pan with a wooden spoon. Once the sauce comes to a simmer, stir in the peanut butter until it dissolves, then stir in the broth. Return the chicken and any accumulated juices to the pan. Bring the stew to a simmer, cover, reduce the heat to very low, and simmer slowly until the chicken is cooked through and the stew is thick, about 30 minutes, stirring often to prevent scorching.

4. Just before serving, stir the vinegar and salt, if using, into the stew. To serve, place ½ cup of cooked rice in each of 4 soup bowls; top each with 2 chicken thighs and one-quarter of the sauce.

Customize It!

For a hotter Madras-style curry, omit all the dried spices and in their stead add this mixture: 2 teaspoons ground ginger, 1 teaspoon ground coriander, 1 teaspoon ground cumin, ½ teaspoon ground cinnamon, ½ teaspoon dry mustard, and ¼ teaspoon cayenne pepper.

For an even hotter, Vindaloo-inspired curry, omit all the dried spices and in their stead add: 1 teaspoon turmeric, 1 teaspoon ground cinnamon, 1 teaspoon ground coriander, 1 teaspoon freshly ground black pepper, ½ teaspoon red pepper flakes, ½ teaspoon ground cumin, ½ teaspoon ground ginger, ½ teaspoon ground cardamom, ¼ teaspoon ground cloves, and ¼ teaspoon cayenne pepper.

For a Thai-inspired curry, omit all the dried spices and add 1 to 2 teaspoons red Thai curry paste (see page 12). Also add 2 tablespoons minced peeled fresh ginger with the garlic. Add 2 tablespoons fish sauce (see page 9) with the tomato sauce.

To make a creamier stew, stir 1 cup sour cream or yogurt (regular, low-fat, or nonfat) into the stew with the vinegar, once the pot is off the heat.

FILIPINO OXTAIL STEW

Oxtails have made a culinary comeback in the past few years—and no won-der: what a sybaritic feast as you suck the juicy meat off the bones! Many cultures, from Dutch to South African, have ways to cook these tender bits, but none uses peanut butter like this traditional stew from the Philippines.

MAKES 8 SERVINGS

1 tablespoon white rice

2 tablespoons peanut oil

4 pounds oxtail segments

2 large whole shallots (both halves of the bulb from each), minced

4 large garlic cloves, minced

4 medium Roma tomatoes, roughly chopped (see Note)

5 cups beef broth, preferably no-salt-added, nonfat broth

¼ cup fish sauce (see page 9)

2 bay leaves

½ cup creamy natural peanut butter

¾ pound green beans, cut into 1-inch pieces (about 2½ cups)

1. Toast the rice in a small nonstick skillet set over low heat until golden and very aromatic, about 3 minutes, shaking the pan constantly to avoid burning the rice. Cool off the heat about 5 minutes, then place in a clean spice grinder or cof-fee grinder and grind the toasted rice into a powder; this will later be used as a condiment on top of the dish.

2. Position the rack in the center of the oven and preheat the oven to 350°F.

3. Heat a large Dutch oven over medium heat. (If it has nonmetal handles, wrap them in aluminum foil to protect them from the oven's heat later on.) Swirl in the peanut oil, wait a couple of seconds, then add about half the oxtail segments.

Brown them on all sides, turning often with metal tongs, about 4 minutes, then transfer them to a large plate and continue cooking the remaining oxtail segments in the same way. Set the browned oxtails aside.

4. Add the shallots and cook, stirring often, until softened, about 30 seconds. Add the garlic, cook for 10 seconds, then stir in the tomatoes. Continue cooking just until they begin to break down, about 20 seconds. Pour in the broth and fish sauce. Stir well with a wooden spoon to scrape up any browned bits on the bottom of the pan, then return the oxtails to the pot and tuck in the bay leaves. Bring the sauce to a simmer, cover the pan, and place it in the oven to bake until the oxtail meat is fork-tender, about 1 hour and 45 minutes.

5. Remove the pot from the oven (be careful of escaping steam and hot, slippery handles). Use a slotted spoon to transfer the oxtails to a large platter. Be gentle because they're tender and you want to keep the meat on the bones. Skim the sauce for any fat (there may be up to 1 cup), then stir in the peanut butter and green beans. Return the oxtails to the pot, cover it again, and place it in the oven for another 30 minutes, until the meat is falling off the bones.

6. To serve, discard the bay leaves. Use a large spoon to lift the oxtails and green beans out of the stew and put them into deep soup bowls. Cover with sauce, then sprinkle about ¼ teaspoon toasted rice powder over each bowl.

NOTE: *For a more aesthetic look, you can seed the tomatoes, too. Cut them into wedges, then use your fingers or a small spoon to dig out the inner membranes and seeds. Discard these and chop the remaining parts of the tomato.*

Customize It!

For a hotter stew, add ¼ to ½ teaspoon cayenne pepper or 1 teaspoon chili paste (see page 7) to the pot with the fish sauce, or serve the dish with Tabasco sauce on the side.

Substitute any of the following for the green beans: broccoli florets, cauliflower florets, or asparagus spears, cut into 2-inch segments.

Add ½ pound of any greens, stemmed and roughly chopped, to the pot after you've skimmed the fat. Consider hearty, flavorful greens such as collard greens, kale, mustard greens, or Swiss chard.

MUSSELS STEAMED IN A COCONUT AND PEANUT CURRY SAUCE

Check the freshness of mussels in two ways: 1) they should smell clean, not fishy or swampy; and 2) any open mussels should close when tapped (discard any that do not). When you get them home, store them in a large bowl in your refrigerator, covered loosely with damp paper towels, for no more than 12 hours. This recipe can easily be doubled or tripled at will.

MAKES 2 SERVINGS

2 pounds fresh mussels

1 tablespoon peanut oil

1 medium onion, chopped

1 tablespoon minced peeled fresh ginger

1 tablespoon green Thai curry paste (see page 12)

½ cup coconut milk, preferably light coconut milk (see page 8)

2 tablespoons fish sauce (see page 9)

2 tablespoons creamy standard peanut butter

1. Wash the mussels thoroughly, scrubbing off any sand or impurities that cling to their shells. Debeard them by pulling out the wiry filaments that protrude from the openings in their shells; once you do this, the mussels will die, so now work quickly through the recipe to get them cooked.

2. Heat a large nonstick wok or a large, deep saucepan over medium-high heat. Pour in the peanut oil, wait for 5 seconds, then add the onion, ginger, and green Thai curry paste. Sauté for 30 seconds, just until the onion softens a bit.

3. Stir in the coconut milk, fish sauce, and peanut butter until the sauce is smooth. Add the mussels, stir well, and bring the sauce to a simmer. Cover the wok or the saucepan, reduce the heat to medium-low, and cook just until the mussels open and expose the inner meat, 3 to 4 minutes. Discard any mussels that don't open. Toss well and serve with lots of crusty bread on hand to scoop up the sauce. Make sure you have a bowl to toss the shells in while you eat the dish.

Customize It!

For a sweeter sauce, add 1 tablespoon packed dark brown sugar with the fish sauce.

For a hotter sauce, use red Thai curry paste rather than green.

Reduce the mussels to 1 pound and add 1 pound scrubbed clams or ½ pound medium shrimp (about 30 per pound), peeled and deveined with the remaining mussels (see page 101 for tips on how to deal with the shrimp).

This same sauce works well for soft-shell crabs. Cut four of them into quarters, then add them to the sauce. Cover and cook until tender, about 3 minutes.

PAD THAI

There may be no more classic peanut butter dish than this sweet-hot Thai noodle concoction that's become something of a new American staple. It's best the moment it's made, when the flavors are bright and intense, so have the ingredients prepped in advance and be ready to sit down with a good beer the moment the dish comes out of the wok.

MAKES 4 SERVINGS

8 ounces dried rice or rice stick noodles

⅓ cup chunky natural peanut butter

¼ cup fish sauce (see page 9)

2 tablespoons hoisin (see page 9)

2 tablespoons rice vinegar (see page 11)

2 tablespoons sugar

1 teaspoon chili paste (see page 7)

2 tablespoons peanut oil

4 medium scallions, cut into 1-inch pieces

4 medium garlic cloves, minced

1 pound medium shrimp, about 30 per pound, peeled and deveined (see Note)

¼ pound bean sprouts (about 1½ cups)

¼ cup packed fresh cilantro leaves, chopped

2 tablespoons lime juice

1. Cover the noodles with hot tap water in a large bowl and soak for 10 minutes. Drain in a colander, rinse with warm water, and set aside while you make the sauce.

2. Whisk the peanut butter, fish sauce, hoisin, rice vinegar, sugar, and chili paste in a medium bowl until creamy; set aside.

3. Heat a large nonstick wok or a large nonstick sauté pan over medium-high heat. Swirl in the oil, wait a couple of seconds, then add the scallions. Stir-fry until slightly softened, about 1 minute; then add the garlic and continue stir-frying until fragrant, about 15 seconds.

4. Add the shrimp and stir-fry until pink, about 2 minutes. Add the bean sprouts and continue stir-frying for 1 minute. Pour in the prepared peanut butter sauce, then the prepared, drained noodles. Toss and cook until bubbly, about 1 minute; then stir in the cilantro and lime juice just before you dish it up.

NOTE: *Peel a shrimp by turning it so the legs face you. Gently pry the legs apart, bending the shell into an arc until it splits between the legs. Grab the extreme end of the tail and gently but firmly pull it free of the meat. Then peel off the shell intact.*

The so-called "vein" running down the shrimp is actually its digestive tract, often full of impurities. To remove the vein, use a knife to make a small slit along the convex curve of the shrimp's "back," then pull out the vein. If the vein splits, use the tip of the knife to pick out the pieces.

Of course, you can avoid all this mess by asking the fishmonger to peel and devein the shrimp for you.

PEANUT BUTTER AND APRICOT GLAZED HAM

Hams glazed with all sorts of sweet concoctions are something of a tradition in the South—and so why not with a peanut butter sauce, one that celebrates one of the region's most famous products?

MAKES 12 SERVINGS

One 10- to 12-pound cooked smoked ham
1 cup apricot jam
½ cup creamy natural peanut butter
½ cup water
¼ cup dark rum, such as Myers's
¼ cup cognac or brandy
3 tablespoons lemon juice
1 tablespoon dry mustard
2 teaspoons ground ginger
1 teaspoon ground cloves

1. Position the rack in the lower third of the oven and preheat the oven to 300°F.

2. Remove the skin from the ham and all but a thin layer of fat surrounding the meat. Place the ham in a large roasting pan. If desired, you can place the ham on a rack to lift it out of the fat that inevitably will drip off while it cooks. Bake until an instant-read meat thermometer inserted into the thickest part of the ham (but not touching the bone) registers 140°F, 2 to 2½ hours. If you've bought a spiral-sliced ham, it will cook faster than one that's not so cut. In any event, cover the ham with foil during the baking if it begins to brown darkly as it cooks.

3. While the ham is baking, place the apricot jam, peanut butter, water, rum, cognac or brandy, lemon juice, dry mustard, ginger, and cloves in a large blender or a food processor fitted with the chopping blade. Blend or process until smooth, scraping down the sides of the canister or bowl as necessary.

4. When the ham's temperature reaches 140°F, remove it from the oven and spread the peanut butter glaze over it. If you have a spiral-sliced ham, separate the slices just slightly so that you get the glaze into them a little bit, perhaps ½ inch. Return the ham to the oven and continue baking until the internal temperature reaches 150°F, basting the ham with the sauce in the pan every 5 minutes. Do not cover it with foil at this point—you want it to get golden brown. Let the ham stand at room temperature for 10 minutes before serving.

Customize It!

Substitute orange marmalade for the apricot jam.

Omit the brandy and use ½ cup rum.

Substitute ½ cup Dr Pepper for the rum and brandy.

Add ¼ teaspoon cayenne pepper with the spices to the food processor.

Substitute ¼ cup prepared mustard, preferably a grainy mustard, for the lemon juice and dry mustard.

PEANUT BUTTER POTSTICKERS

These tender, light dumplings are made with shrimp and a little peanut sauce, then fried in toasted sesame oil for a crunchy outside that contrasts well with the creamy filling. Serve them with the simple dipping sauce that follows.

MAKES 24 DUMPLINGS (ABOUT 8 APPETIZER OR 4 MAIN-COURSE SERVINGS)

3 scallions, thinly sliced

1 large garlic clove, minced

2 tablespoons minced peeled fresh ginger

2 tablespoons chunky natural peanut butter

1 teaspoon rice vinegar (see page 11)

½ teaspoon five spice powder

½ pound medium shrimp (about 30 per pound), peeled and deveined (see
    page 101 for tips on how to do this)

24 dumpling wrappers

2 tablespoons toasted sesame oil (see page 12)

1½ cups water

1. Place the scallions, garlic, ginger, peanut butter, rice vinegar, and five spice powder in a food processor fitted with the chopping blade; pulse three or four times until well blended. Scrape down the sides of the bowl with a rubber spatula, then add the shrimp and pulse several times to chop and blend, until the mixture resembles a very thick, chunky salsa.

2. Fill a custard cup or teacup with water and place it near your work surface. Lay a dumpling wrapper on the work surface. Place about 1 rounded teaspoon of filling in the center of a wrapper. Dip your finger in the water, then run it halfway around the rim of the wrapper. Seal the dumpling, pressing the wet rim against the dry. Starting at the right end and working to the left, crimp the edges closed by folding the sealed edge in ¼-inch increments over itself, thereby creating the look of a small leather purse. Set aside and continue making the dumplings. (The dumplings can be made in advance—place them on a large baking sheet dusted with cornstarch, seal tightly with plastic wrap, and store in the refrigerator for up to 1 day.)

3. Heat a large skillet over medium heat. Add 1 tablespoon sesame oil, then place 12 dumplings in the skillet, laying them on their sides. Fry until brown on that side without turning, about 2 minutes. Then pour ¾ cup water into the skillet, cover, raise the heat to high, and cook for 3 minutes. Uncover the skillet, shake it to make sure the dumplings are not stuck, and continue cooking until the water has completely evaporated and the bottoms are crisp, about 1 more minute. Transfer them to a platter, then make a second batch with the remaining dumplings, following the same method described in this step. When done, serve the dumplings with the Dumpling Dipping Sauce (recipe follows).

DUMPLING DIPPING SAUCE

> 3 tablespoons reduced-sodium soy sauce
>
> 3 tablespoons rice vinegar (see page 11)
>
> 1½ teaspoons lemon juice
>
> ½ teaspoon chili paste (see page 7)

Mix the ingredients in a small bowl until well combined; serve with the dumplings as a dip.

PEANUT BUTTER TERIYAKI CHICKEN

Peanut butter adds a spiky taste to this traditionally sweet Japanese dish. You can marinate the chicken breasts all day while you're at work, then pop them under the broiler when you come home for a quick, easy dinner. Have lots of white or brown rice on hand, or serve the glazed breasts with a vinegary salad of lettuce, tomatoes, broccoli florets, and sprouts.

MAKES 8 SERVINGS

½ cup soy sauce, preferably reduced-sodium soy sauce

¼ cup honey (see page 10)

¼ cup creamy natural peanut butter

2 tablespoons mirin (see page 10)

1 tablespoon minced peeled fresh ginger

1 large garlic clove, minced

Eight (4-ounce) boneless, skinless chicken breasts

1. Whisk the soy sauce, honey, peanut butter, mirin, ginger, and garlic in a shallow glass baking dish until smooth. Add the chicken breasts and toss well to coat. Cover the bowl with plastic wrap and refrigerate at least 3 hours, or up to 8 hours, turning occasionally so that the chicken is thoroughly coated in the marinade.

2. Line your broiler pan with aluminum foil to make cleanup easier. Place the pan 4 to 5 inches from the heat source and preheat the broiler for 5 minutes. Place the chicken breasts on the broiler pan and broil until firm to the touch and cooked through, about 10 minutes, turning once. An instant-read meat thermometer inserted into the thickest part of the breast meat should read 165°F. Transfer the cooked breasts to a serving platter and let stand for 5 minutes before serving to let the juices reincorporate into the meat.

Grill Them!

This dish is excellent on the grill, over either direct or indirect heat. If you use direct heat, prepare the grill as suggested by the manufacturer's instructions, then place the chicken breasts directly over the flame or the coal bed; grill until cooked through and browned, about 8 minutes, turning once. If you use indirect heat, prepare a hot coal bed to one side of the grill or turn on only one section of a gas grill. Place the breasts on the other side of the grill, away from the heat, and close the lid; barbecue for about 15 minutes, turning once.

Customize Them!

Substitute an equivalent amount of frozen juice concentrate, such as apple, cranberry, orange, or pineapple, thawed, for the honey.

PEANUT LAMB CURRY

Here's a spicy lamb stew, reminiscent of a classic Indian curry, thickened with yogurt and peanut butter—ever so creamy and rich. Frankly, it's a meal in itself, but you might want to serve it with a cool salad of sliced tomatoes and chopped basil dressed with a little vinaigrette. Have lots of white rice on hand to balance the spicy flavors.

MAKES 4 SERVINGS

2 tablespoons peanut oil

1 pound boneless lamb shoulder, cut into 1-inch cubes

4 medium onions, halved, each half cut into 3 wedges

2 large garlic cloves, minced

2½ teaspoons ground ginger

2 teaspoons ground coriander

1 teaspoon ground cinnamon

½ teaspoon salt

¼ teaspoon cayenne pepper, or less to taste

⅛ teaspoon ground cloves

¼ cup dry vermouth, dry white wine, or water

¾ cup plain yogurt (regular, low-fat, or fat free)

¼ cup creamy natural peanut butter

¼ cup golden raisins

1. Heat a large Dutch oven over medium heat, then add the oil followed by the lamb chunks. Cook just until they are browned all over, about 4 minutes, turning often. (You may work in batches, if necessary.) Transfer the lamb to a large platter; set aside.

2. Add the onions to the pot and sauté until lightly browned, about 3 minutes. Add the garlic, cook for 10 seconds, then sprinkle in the ginger, coriander, cinnamon, salt, cayenne, and cloves. Stir well, cook about 10 more seconds, then pour in the vermouth, wine, or water to deglaze the pot. Scrape up any browned bits on the bottom of the pan, then add the meat along with the yogurt, peanut butter, and raisins, stirring until the peanut butter dissolves. Cover the pot, reduce the heat to very low, and simmer slowly until the meat is very tender when pierced with a fork, about 40 minutes, stirring often to prevent scorching. Set aside, covered, for 5 minutes off the heat, then serve at once.

Customize It!

You can omit all the dried spices and use one of the curry mixtures on pages 93–94.

Omit the cayenne for a sweeter, milder stew.

Substitute pork stew meat or 1 pound pork loin, cut into 2-inch pieces, for the lamb.

Substitute 1 pound skinless chicken thighs for the lamb—cook just until they are tender, about 20 minutes.

SATAY

"**S**atay" actually refers to a culinary technique: skewering bits of meat or vegetables, grilling them, and serving them with a piquant peanut sauce. Truly the street food of Indonesia, it's served up at all hours by vendors from their kitchens on wheels. At your house, serve it as a main course with steamed green beans, or as an appetizer at your next cocktail party (for ideas about drinks at that party, see our *Ultimate Party Drink Book*).

MAKES 4 SERVINGS

1½ pounds sirloin steak, cut into 16 strips (about ¼ inch thick) against the grain (see Note)

¼ cup plus 1 tablespoon peanut oil

1 teaspoon ground cinnamon

1 teaspoon ground coriander

1 teaspoon ground ginger

1 teaspoon dry mustard

½ teaspoon garlic powder

½ teaspoon freshly ground black pepper

½ cup creamy natural peanut butter

6 tablespoons soy sauce, preferably reduced-sodium soy sauce

¼ cup rice vinegar (see page 11)

2 teaspoons sugar

Sixteen 10-inch bamboo skewers, soaked in water for 20 minutes

1. Place the steak strips in a large bowl. Pour in 1 tablespoon peanut oil, then add the ground cinnamon, ground coriander, ground ginger, dry mustard, garlic powder, and ground black pepper. Toss well, cover, and place in the refrigerator to marinate at least 1 hour or up to 10 hours.

2. Whisk the peanut butter, soy sauce, rice vinegar, sugar, and the remaining ¼ cup peanut oil in a medium bowl until smooth; set aside as the dipping sauce for the satay.

3. Take one of the sirloin strips and thread it onto one of the skewers by weaving the skewer back and forth through the meat, starting at one short end and finishing at the other, thereby piercing the piece of meat three or four times with the skewer to keep it solidly attached. Keep the meat close to one end of the skewer so that the other end becomes a long handle for the satay. Set on a platter and repeat with all the skewers and steak strips.

4. Prepare the barbecue grill or preheat the broiler with the broiler pan about 4 inches from the heat source. You may want to wrap the exposed, long handles of the skewers in aluminum foil to protect them from the heat.

5. Grill or broil the meat about 3 minutes, turning once, until medium-rare, juicy, still soft, and very fragrant. (The meat should feel like the lax skin between your thumb and index finger when pressed.) Unwrap the skewers if you've guarded them with aluminum foil and serve with the prepared peanut dipping sauce on the side.

NOTE: *Cutting meat against the grain is fairly easy once you get the hang of it. Lay the steak on a clean cutting board and run your fingers across it, pressing down a bit. You'll eventually see which way the fibers are running, usually at an angle in the steak. Cut the steak at a 90-degree angle to these fibers so the pieces stay together in strips.*

Customize It!

Of course, you can use chicken strips, peeled and deveined medium shrimp (about 30 per pound—see page 101 for tips on dealing with shrimp), pork loin strips, or even pieces of firm tofu or seitan to make satay. Thread them on the skewers as indicated. You can probably fit 3 shrimp per skewer; bend them open, so they're uncurved, as it were, as straight as possible, as you thread them onto the skewers; this way, they'll stay elongated as they cook.

Heat up the dipping sauce by whisking ½ to 1 teaspoon chili paste into the peanut dipping sauce.

Serve these skewers over Cucumber Noodles (page 72) for a wonderful lunch or easy dinner.

SENEGALESE PEANUT STEW

Peanuts have long been a part of African cooking, thanks mostly to Spanish and Portuguese traders. This vegetarian soup takes advantage of the traditional chile and clove blends that dominate Senegalese cooking.

MAKES 8 SERVINGS

2 tablespoons peanut oil

2 medium onions, roughly chopped

1 large sweet potato (about 1 pound), preferably a white sweet potato, peeled and chopped into ½-inch cubes

2 carrots, thinly sliced

2 garlic cloves, minced

2 tablespoons minced peeled fresh ginger

¾ teaspoon ground cloves

½ teaspoon salt, optional

¼ teaspoon cayenne pepper, or less to taste

4 cups vegetable broth, preferably no-salt broth

1 cup creamy natural peanut butter

1. Heat a large saucepan over medium heat. Pour in the oil, wait a second or two, then add the onions and cook, stirring frequently, until softened and golden, about 2 minutes. Add the sweet potato chunks, carrots, and garlic; cook, stirring, for 30 seconds.

2. Sprinkle in the ginger, cloves, salt, if using, and cayenne; cook for 10 seconds, then pour in the vegetable broth. Bring the mixture to a simmer, scraping up any browned bits on the bottom of the pan with a wooden spoon. Stir in the peanut butter until smooth. Cover, reduce the heat to low, and simmer until the sweet potato chunks are tender and the soup is quite thick, about 30 minutes, stirring often to prevent scorching. Cool for 5 minutes off the heat before serving.

Customize It!

Stir ½ pound collard greens, mustard greens, turnip greens, kale, or Swiss chard, all stemmed and roughly chopped, into the soup with the peanut butter.

Serve the stew with African flatbread, Indian na'an, or even flour tortillas—use them to scoop up the stew as you eat it.

Serve the stew accompanied by a cooling mixture of plain yogurt and diced cucumbers.

SZECHWAN STIR-FRY

Szechwan restaurants in New York City have recently started a foodie fad for sizzling-sweet chicken dishes made with zucchini and chili sauce. But they would have an even bigger trend on their hands if they just used peanut butter! Szechwan peppercorns, actually a citrus product, are now banned in the U.S., but you can still find holdout bags in Asian markets if you look carefully. If you can't find them, sprinkle 1 teaspoon Szechwan peppercorn oil on the dish just before it comes out of the wok.

MAKES 4 SERVINGS

- 3 tablespoons chunky natural peanut butter
- 3 tablespoons soy sauce, preferably reduced-sodium soy sauce
- 2 tablespoons black vinegar (see page 7), or 1 tablespoon balsamic vinegar and 1 tablespoon Worcestershire sauce
- 2 teaspoons chili paste (see page 7)
- 1 teaspoon sugar
- 1 tablespoon peanut oil
- 3 scallions, finely chopped
- 4 medium garlic cloves, minced
- 2 tablespoons minced peeled fresh ginger
- 1 pound boneless, skinless chicken thighs, cut into 1½-inch pieces
- 2 small zucchini, roughly chopped
- 1 teaspoon Szechwan peppercorns
- 2 cups cooked white or brown rice

1. Whisk the peanut butter, soy sauce, black vinegar, chili paste, and sugar in a small bowl until smooth; set aside.

2. Heat a large nonstick wok or nonstick sauté pan over medium-high heat. Swirl in the oil, then add the scallions, garlic, and ginger. Stir-fry for 30 seconds, then add the chicken. Stir-fry until almost cooked through and lightly browned, about 3 minutes.

3. Add the zucchini and continue cooking, stirring and tossing constantly, just until the zucchini starts to soften, about 1 minute. Pour in the prepared peanut sauce and the Szechwan peppercorns, if using. Cook, stirring frequently, until the sauce is bubbling and thick; the meat should be completely coated in this brown glaze. Place ½ cup cooked rice in each of 4 bowls, divide the stir-fry among them, and serve at once.

Customize It!

Substitute 1 pound medium shrimp (about 30 per pound), peeled and deveined (see page 101 for tips on how to do this), or 1 pound sirloin steak, sliced into ¼-inch-thick strips against the grain (see page 111), for the chicken.

Substitute 2 small cucumbers, fleshy parts cut into matchsticks, seeds and pulp discarded, for the zucchini.

Omit the rice and serve the stir-fry over steamed, wilted mustard greens, turnip greens, or spinach.

THAI STIR-FRY

Since they were traded to Asia over three centuries ago, peanuts have become a boon to local cuisines, but perhaps no more so than to Thai cuisine, known for both its popping heat from chiles and the subtle sweetness of sauces that tame the burn.

MAKES 4 SERVINGS

2 pounds boneless, skinless chicken breasts, cut into 2-inch pieces

3 large garlic cloves, minced

2 tablespoons chopped peeled fresh ginger

1 teaspoon red Thai curry paste (see page 12)

2 tablespoons vegetable oil

4 medium scallions, cut into 1-inch pieces

1 medium red bell pepper, cored, seeded, and diced

1 small red onion, minced (about ½ cup)

¼ teaspoon red pepper flakes

1 tablespoon sugar

½ cup coconut milk, preferably light coconut milk (see page 8)

6 tablespoons chunky natural peanut butter

¼ cup fish sauce (see page 9)

3 tablespoons lime juice

2 cups cooked jasmine rice

1. Place the chicken pieces in a large bowl; toss with the garlic, ginger, and red curry paste. Cover and refrigerate to marinate, at least 1 hour but no more than 10 hours.

2. Heat a large nonstick wok or a large nonstick sauté pan over medium-high heat. Pour in the oil, then add the chicken and all of the spice marinade it's been sitting in. Stir-fry just until the chicken browns slightly, just until it loses its raw, pink look, a little less than 2 minutes. Be careful: the volatilized chili oils from the curry paste can burn your eyes and nose. Transfer the chicken to a large plate and set aside.

3. Add the scallions, bell pepper, and onion to the wok or sauté pan; stir-fry until slightly softened, about 1 minute. Add the red pepper flakes and stir-fry until aromatic, about 10 seconds. Sprinkle the sugar over the vegetables in the pan, then pour in the coconut milk and bring the sauce to a simmer.

4. Return the chicken to the sauce, then stir in the peanut butter until the sauce is silky and smooth. Stir in the fish sauce and lime juice, bring to a full boil, reduce the heat, and simmer until thick and glistening, about 2 minutes. Serve at once, each portion over ½ cup cooked jasmine rice.

VIETNAMESE LETTUCE WRAPS

Forgo the tortillas and make these Southeast Asian wraps the traditional way: with lettuce leaves. Separate and wash the leaves, then pat them dry and store them surrounded by paper towels in sealed plastic bags in your crisper for up to 48 hours, until you're ready to make the dish. You can also make the filling up to a day in advance; store it, covered, in the refrigerator but microwave it warm before serving. Simply offer it alongside the lettuce leaves so everyone can roll their own little bundles.

MAKES 8 SERVINGS

1 tablespoon peanut oil

6 scallions, white and green parts chopped separately and set aside

1 tablespoon plus 2 teaspoons minced peeled fresh ginger

1 large garlic clove, minced

1 pound lean ground beef

¼ cup crunchy standard peanut butter

¼ cup lime juice

3 tablespoons fish sauce (see page 9)

1 teaspoon chili paste (see page 7)

5 radishes, roughly chopped

¼ cup packed fresh cilantro leaves, chopped

¼ cup packed fresh mint leaves, chopped

2 large heads Boston lettuce, leaves washed and separated (about 32 leaves)

1. Heat a large nonstick skillet or wok over medium-high heat. Pour in the peanut oil, wait for a few seconds, then add the chopped white parts of the scallion. Stir-fry for 30 seconds, just to soften, then add 1 tablespoon of the ginger and the garlic. Stir-fry for 15 seconds before crumbling in the ground beef. Continue cooking, stirring constantly, until the meat is browned and cooked through, about 5 minutes. Transfer this mixture to a large bowl and cool for 5 minutes.

2. Meanwhile, whisk the peanut butter, lime juice, fish sauce, chili paste, and the remaining 2 teaspoons minced ginger in a small bowl until smooth.

3. Once the meat mixture has cooled slightly, stir in the prepared peanut butter sauce as well as the radishes, cilantro, and mint.

4. To serve, place about 2 tablespoons of this filling in a lettuce leaf, then roll it closed and enjoy.

More Ideas

Omit the Boston lettuce and use at least 4 heads Belgian endive; spoon a teaspoon or so of the mixture into each of the spears for an elegant appetizer.

Use the filling as a dip much like a Brazilian peccadillo. Use tortilla chips to scoop it up.

Snacks

Sometimes, you just have a hankering for peanut butter. And while spreading it on apple slices may well scratch that itch (see page 127 for our ultimate ideas), there are other ways to make a peanut butter–inspired snack that'll get you from cocktails to dinner—or simply get you through the afternoon when the hunger pangs hit.

ELVIS SPREAD

We got the inspiration for this one from the King himself—or from his acclaimed proclivities for peanut butter, banana, and bacon sandwiches.

MAKES 2 CUPS

6 strips thick-cut bacon

1¼ cups creamy standard peanut butter

2 ripe medium bananas, peeled and cut into 2-inch sections

1 tablespoon unsalted butter, at room temperature

1 tablespoon honey (see page 10)

1. Fry the bacon in a nonstick skillet set over medium-high heat until the strips are very crispy, about 4 minutes, turning occasionally. Transfer the bacon slices to a paper towel–lined plate and blot the strips dry with more paper towels. Set aside.

2. Place the peanut butter, bananas, butter, and honey in a food processor fitted with the chopping blade. Process until very smooth, scraping down the sides of the bowl as necessary.

3. Chop the bacon, then add it to the food processor and pulse two or three times to get it evenly distributed in the mixture. Scoop the spread into a bowl or container, cover tightly, and store in the refrigerator for up to 4 days; bring the spread to room temperature before using.

PEANUT BUTTER HUMMUS

Hummus is a traditional Middle Eastern chickpea spread, often put on flat-bread or served as a dip for vegetables, or sometimes used like mayo or mustard on a sandwich. Although this peanut butter variety might not garner any awards for authenticity, it's sure to win compliments at your next party.

MAKES ABOUT 1½ CUPS

One 15-ounce can chickpeas, drained and rinsed

1 large garlic clove, chopped

½ cup lemon juice

¼ cup creamy natural peanut butter

1 teaspoon ground cumin

3 to 4 dashes Tabasco sauce, or more to taste

Place the chickpeas, garlic, lemon juice, peanut butter, and cumin in a food processor fitted with the chopping blade. Process until smooth. Add the Tabasco sauce to taste, pulse once or twice to incorporate, and scoop the mixture into a serving bowl or a storage container. The hummus may be kept tightly covered in the refrigerator for up to 3 days.

Customize It!

Substitute 1 teaspoon yellow or red curry powder for the cumin.

Add 1 teaspoon onion powder, ½ teaspoon ground cinnamon, ½ teaspoon ground ginger, or ½ teaspoon garam masala with the cumin.

Reduce the lemon juice to ¼ cup; add 1 yellow bell pepper, cored and seeded, or 1 large jarred pimiento with the other ingredients.

PEANUT BUTTER PROTEIN SNACK BARS

Don't pay all that money for protein bars, especially when you can make your own without any chemical preservatives. Wrapped individually, these will keep for 2 weeks at room temperature. Carry them in your gym bag, work tote, purse, or backpack.

MAKES 12 BARS

Nonstick spray

¾ cup packed light brown sugar

½ cup light corn syrup

¼ cup honey (see page 10)

1 cup creamy natural peanut butter

1 tablespoon vanilla extract

3½ cups purchased granola cereal

1 cup powdered nonfat dry milk

¼ cup unflavored soy protein powder (see Note)

1. Lightly spray a 9 × 13-inch baking pan with nonstick spray; set aside.

2. Mix the brown sugar, corn syrup, and honey in a small saucepan and set it over medium heat. Bring the mixture to a simmer, stirring until the sugar dissolves. Boil for 2 minutes undisturbed, then remove the pan from the heat, and stir in the peanut butter and vanilla.

3. Pour the peanut butter mixture into a large bowl. Add the granola cereal, powdered dry milk, and soy protein powder. Beat with an electric mixer at medium speed until uniform and fairly cohesive. Gather the stiff, taffy-like mixture into a ball and press it into the prepared pan. Place the pan on a wire rack and cool completely, about 1 hour.

4. Turn the entire protein bar block out onto a cutting board, then use a large knife to slice it into 16 rectangular bars; cut it once down the center, then turn the block 90 degrees and cut each half into 8 bars. Wrap the bars individually in plastic wrap and store in an airtight container at room temperature for up to 2 weeks.

NOTE: *Unsweetened unflavored soy protein powder is available at almost all health food stores.*

Customize It!

Stir ¾ cup of any of the following or any mixture of the following into the bar batter during the final few seconds of beating it: chopped dried figs, chopped pecans, chopped pitted dates, chopped unsalted roasted peanuts, chopped walnuts, dried blueberries, dried cherries, dried cranberries, dried currants, mini chocolate chips, and/or raisins.

For a double peanut butter hit, use 3½ cups Peanut Butter Granola (page 32).

PEANUT BUTTER TEA SANDWICHES

These little tea sandwiches are great for whenever you want a bite without a full meal. Or put these out when guests drop by. Don't forget to cut off the crusts!

MAKES 16 LITTLE SANDWICHES

3 tablespoons creamy natural peanut butter

2 tablespoons finely chopped crystallized ginger

1 tablespoon mayonnaise

2 teaspoons lemon juice

8 slices white or country white bread

1. Mash the peanut butter into the ginger, mayonnaise, and lemon juice in a medium bowl, then mix until smooth. (The spread can be made up to 3 days in advance; cover and refrigerate, then bring to room temperature before proceeding.)

2. Spread about 1½ tablespoons onto 4 of the slices of bread. Top with the other 4 slices. Cut off the crusts, then cut the sandwiches in half corner to corner, thereby making 8 triangular sandwiches. Cut each of these in half from the widest-angle corner to the middle of the longest side, thereby making a total of 16 little triangular sandwiches. Serve at once, or place on a plate, cover with plastic wrap, and let stand at room temperature for up to 1 hour.

Customize It!

Stir a few dashes of Tabasco sauce into the peanut butter mixture.

Layer thinly sliced cucumbers, radishes, or watercress on the peanut butter spread before you close the sandwiches.

THE ULTIMATE PEANUT BUTTER VEHICLES

Most everybody wants a quick snack from time to time—just peanut butter spread on something. Here's a list of our ultimate favorites, ways to enjoy crunchy or creamy peanut butter without a lot of fuss or fanfare.

- on a finger (or a spoon, if you insist), then dipped in chocolate syrup, caramel sauce, jam, honey, Marshmallow Fluff, or Marshmallow Crème
- on apple wedges
- on baby carrots
- on banana halves
- on celery
- on chocolate bars
- on chocolate chip cookies
- on dried apples, then dotted with raisins
- on fruit leather
- on melba toast with a dot of mango chutney
- on pear wedges
- on pitted dates, topped with a dab of softened cream cheese
- on prunes, then sprinkled with cocoa nibs
- on rice cakes
- on rice crackers, then topped with dried cranberries or chopped dried figs
- on saltines or other crackers
- on thick-cut waffle potato chips
- on toast or even buttered toast
- on toasted bagels or English muffins
- on tortillas—add some jam, roll them up, and make a breakfast burrito
- on vanilla wafer cookies, sprinkled with chocolate chips
- on waffles, topped with maple syrup

Drinks

We all know the pleasures of a glass of milk and a peanut butter sandwich, so it's a natural that milk (or, well, ice cream) and peanut butter make a yummy cocktail or a refreshing smoothie.

Making Blender Drinks

For the best drinks, "soften" the ice. In other words, leave it out on the counter for a few minutes. That way, you'll get a smoother drink without those pesky shards.

For these drinks, the ingredients are listed in the order in which you put them into the blender. That's because of a common mistake home bartenders make with frozen drinks: they put the ice on the top, not on the bottom with the blades. In doing so, they inadvertently make chunky drinks with random ice chips. We recommend the method preferred by professional bartenders: put the ice in first and let the other ingredients weigh it down onto the blades, with the peanut butter most often coming last in the mix.

Don't hesitate to let the blender run. The drink should be slushy and well combined—and that usually takes 30 seconds, maybe a minute, and sometimes even a little more.

CHOCOLATE PEANUT BUTTER RASPBERRY FREEZE

Here's a cocktail version of a candy we all love: a chocolate peanut butter cup—that is, if you topped it with raspberry jam.

MAKES 2 DRINKS

1 cup ice

⅔ cup chocolate ice cream

¼ cup (2 ounces) raspberry liqueur, such as Chambord

2 tablespoons (1 ounce) brandy

2 tablespoons chocolate syrup

2 tablespoons milk, preferably nonfat

¼ cup creamy standard peanut butter

Place the ingredients in the order listed in a large blender. Blend until smooth, making sure that the ice is completely crushed in the mix. Pour into 2 glasses and serve at once.

Without the Buzz?

Omit the raspberry liqueur and brandy. Increase the ice cream to ¾ cup and add 2 tablespoons raspberry jam with the peanut butter.

Customize It!

Substitute butter pecan, strawberry, or vanilla fudge swirl ice cream for the chocolate ice cream.

Substitute purchased ice cream caramel sauce for the chocolate syrup.

Substitute a coffee-flavored liqueur such as Kahlúa for the raspberry liqueur.

FROZEN PEANUT BUTTER BRANDY ALEXANDER

A traditional Brandy Alexander is made of brandy, crème de cacao, and cream, served in martini glasses. With ice cream and peanut butter, it's pure bliss.

MAKES 2 MARTINI-STYLE DRINKS

½ cup ice

1 cup vanilla ice cream

3 tablespoons (1½ ounces) brandy

3 tablespoons (1½ ounces) white crème de cacao

3 tablespoons creamy standard peanut butter

¼ teaspoon vanilla extract

Pinch of grated nutmeg

Place the ingredients in the order listed in a large blender; blend until smooth, making sure the ice cream and ice are thoroughly incorporated into the drink. Pour into 2 martini glasses and serve at once.

Customize It!

Substitute butter pecan or chocolate ice cream for the vanilla ice cream.

Substitute bourbon, cognac, or Southern Comfort for the brandy.

Add ½ teaspoon ground cinnamon with the vanilla.

FROZEN PEANUT BUTTER WHITE RUSSIAN

A White Russian is a vodka, Kahlúa, and cream cocktail. With peanut butter and vanilla ice cream, it's a frozen indulgence worthy of your next party (or the Czar).

MAKES 2 DRINKS

1 cup ice

¼ cup (2 ounces) coffee-flavored liqueur, such as Kahlúa

¼ cup (2 ounces) vodka

⅔ cup vanilla ice cream

3 tablespoons creamy standard peanut butter

½ teaspoon vanilla extract

Place the ingredients in the order listed in a large blender; blend until smooth, scraping down the sides of the canister as necessary to get the ice evenly pulverized. Pour into 2 glasses and serve at once.

Without the Buzz?

Omit the coffee-flavored liqueur and the vodka; increase the ice cream to ¾ cup and add ¼ cup brewed, cooled espresso, ⅓ cup very strong coffee, or 2 tablespoons coffee syrup after the vodka.

Customize It!

Substitute banana, butter pecan, chocolate, or coffee ice cream for the vanilla ice cream. While it's no longer a Russian if you take out the coffee-flavored liqueur, you can substitute a range of liqueurs. Our favorites include ginger-flavored liqueur such as The Original Canton, hazelnut-flavored liqueur such as Frangelico, or caramel schnapps.

PEANUT BUTTER APPLE PIE COOLER

This cocktail is as much dessert as an afternoon treat. Serve it when you want to kick back and take in the sunset.

MAKES 2 DRINKS

¾ cup ice

1 cup vanilla ice cream

6 tablespoons (3 ounces) apple schnapps

¼ cup creamy standard peanut butter

¼ teaspoon ground cinnamon

Place the ingredients in the order listed in a large blender; blend until smooth. Pour into 2 tumblers and serve at once.

Without the Buzz?

Increase the ice to 1 cup and add ¼ cup milk and either ½ cup purchased apple pie filling or apple butter with the peanut butter.

Customize It!

Reduce the apple schnapps to ¼ cup (2 ounces) and add 2 tablespoons (1 ounce) caramel or cinnamon schnapps, ginger-flavored liqueur such as The Original Canton, or hazelnut-flavored liqueur such as Frangelico.

PEANUT BUTTER AVALANCHE

This thick, malted, vanilla cocktail is perfect for a summer deck party—just have lots of ice on hand so you can make several rounds.

MAKES 2 DRINKS

1 cup ice

⅔ cup vanilla ice cream

¼ cup (2 ounces) vanilla-flavored liqueur, such as Cuarente y Tres (Licor 43)

2 tablespoons (1 ounce) vodka

¼ cup malted milk powder

¼ cup creamy standard peanut butter

¼ cup milk, preferably nonfat

Place the ingredients in the order listed in a blender; blend until smooth, making sure the ice cubes get thoroughly crushed up in the mix. Pour into 2 glasses and serve at once.

Almond Peanut Butter Avalanche Substitute an almond-flavored liqueur such as Amaretto for the vanilla-flavored liqueur; add ½ teaspoon ground cinnamon with the milk.

Peanut Butter Chocolate Avalanche Substitute a chocolate-flavored liqueur such as Godiva for the vanilla-flavored liqueur.

Without the Buzz?

Omit the vanilla-flavored liqueur and the vodka; increase the ice cream to ¾ cup and add 1 tablespoon vanilla extract with it.

PEANUT BUTTER CHOCOLATE EGG CREAM

Egg creams are a New York classic—but not with peanut butter . . . until now. Any New Yorker knows there's no egg or cream in an egg cream. Rather, it's a chocolate milk drink made fizzy with seltzer.

MAKES 1 DRINK

2 tablespoons creamy standard peanut butter

¼ cup chocolate syrup

½ cup milk, preferably low-fat or nonfat

1 cup seltzer

Stir the peanut butter and chocolate syrup in the bottom of a 16-ounce tumbler with a long-handled iced-tea spoon until smooth. Stir in the milk until smooth. Add the seltzer, stirring constantly, until the drink develops a fizzy head. Serve at once.

Peanut Butter Coffee Egg Cream Substitute coffee syrup for the chocolate syrup.

Peanut Butter Vanilla Egg Cream Substitute vanilla syrup for the chocolate syrup.

PEANUT BUTTER CHOCOLATE MALT

Talk about the ultimate malt! Try this with your next burger and fries—and put off the diet for one more day.

MAKES 2 DRINKS

1 cup ice

1 cup chocolate ice cream

¾ cup milk, preferably nonfat

¼ cup chocolate syrup

¼ cup creamy standard peanut butter

¼ cup malted milk powder

Place the ingredients in the order listed in a large blender; blend until smooth, scraping down the canister once or twice to make sure everything has blended evenly. Pour into 2 glasses and serve at once.

Peanut Butter Strawberry Malt Substitute strawberry ice cream for the chocolate ice cream; omit the chocolate syrup and add 2 tablespoons strawberry jam in its stead.

Peanut Butter Banana and Chocolate Malt Substitute banana nectar for the milk.

With the Buzz?

Decrease the milk to ½ cup and add ¼ cup (2 ounces) vodka and 2 tablespoons (1 ounce) dark crème de cacao with the chocolate syrup.

PEANUT BUTTER COFFEEHOUSE FROZEN DRINK

Who doesn't love those frozen coffee drinks that have become all the rage? They're cool, refreshing, and best on summer days.

MAKES 2 DRINKS

½ cup ice

1½ tablespoons powdered nonfat dry milk

¼ cup milk, preferably low-fat or nonfat

3 tablespoons dark corn syrup

⅓ cup brewed espresso, cooled (see Note)

2 tablespoons creamy standard peanut butter

¼ teaspoon vanilla extract

Place the ingredients in the order listed in a large blender; blend until smooth. Pour into 2 glasses and serve at once.

NOTE: *If you don't have an espresso maker, make the espresso for this cocktail from 1 tablespoon instant espresso powder dissolved in ⅓ cup water.*

With the Buzz?

Increase the peanut butter to 3 tablespoons and add 3 tablespoons (1½ ounces) vodka or rum with the espresso.

PEANUT BUTTER LHASSI

Alhassi is an East Indian yogurt drink, often served before a meal or midway through to cool you down from all the spicy food. It's also great as a break-fast smoothie before a busy day.

MAKES 1 LARGE DRINK

½ cup ice

¼ cup plus 2 tablespoons yogurt, preferably nonfat

¼ cup orange juice

1 medium mango, peeled, the fruit cut away from the pit and roughly chopped (see Note)

2 tablespoons creamy standard peanut butter

2 tablespoons honey (see page 10)

½ teaspoon vanilla extract

Place the ingredients in the order listed in a large blender; blend until smooth, scraping down the sides of the bowl as necessary. Pour into a large tumbler and serve at once.

NOTE: *The sap from a mango can cause a skin rash in some people. Even the dried residue on the skin can burn those sensitive. Wear rubber gloves to peel mangoes if you've noticed any sensitivity.*

Customize It!

Substitute apple, pineapple, or white grape juice for the orange juice.

Substitute 1 cup chopped fresh pineapple or 1 cup canned crushed pineapple in juice, drained, for the mango.

Add a scoop of unflavored unsweetened protein powder with the peanut butter.

PEANUT BUTTER MALT

Because peanut butter is rich, we feel that the best malted milk is made with nonfat milk. Don't skimp on the malted milk powder; its taste matches beautifully with peanut butter.

MAKES 2 DRINKS

2 cups milk, preferably nonfat

6 tablespoons malted milk powder

¼ cup creamy standard peanut butter

1 tablespoon packed light brown sugar

1 teaspoon vanilla extract

Place the ingredients in a blender and blend until smooth, scraping down the sides of the canister as necessary. Pour into 2 glasses and serve.

Customize It!

Reduce the milk to 1 cup and add 1 cup chocolate, vanilla, or strawberry ice cream.

Omit the brown sugar and add 2 tablespoons caramel ice cream sauce, chocolate sauce, raspberry jam, or strawberry jam in its stead.

PEANUT BUTTER SMOOTHIE

Talk about something to perk you up after a workout! This easy smoothie will take the edge off any lingering hunger—thanks to peanut butter, of course.

MAKES 1 LARGE DRINK

1 ripe banana, peeled and cut into 4 segments

2 tablespoons creamy standard peanut butter

1 teaspoon honey (see page 10)

⅔ cup yogurt, preferably nonfat

¼ cup orange juice

1 teaspoon vanilla extract

¼ teaspoon ground cinnamon

Place the ingredients in a blender in the order listed. Blend until smooth, pour into a large glass, and drink at once.

Customize It!

Substitute 4 large strawberries for the banana.

Substitute ⅓ cup raspberries for the banana.

Omit the honey and vary the smoothie in hundreds of ways by using flavored yogurts such as blueberry, strawberry, or vanilla.

TROPICAL PEANUT BUTTER BLAST

Serve this Polynesian smoothie before any barbecue—or from the tiki bar at your next retro party.

MAKES 2 DRINKS

1 cup ice
½ cup vanilla ice cream
½ cup (4 ounces) coconut rum
⅓ cup mango nectar
1 ripe banana, peeled and cut into 4 pieces
¼ cup creamy standard peanut butter

Place the ingredients in the order listed in a large blender; blend until smooth, scraping down the sides of the canister as necessary to get the ice evenly pulverized. Pour into 2 glasses and serve at once.

Without the Buzz?

Substitute light coconut milk for the coconut rum.

Customize It!

Substitute coconut ice cream or pineapple sherbet for the vanilla ice cream.
Substitute pineapple juice for the mango nectar.

Cookies

It's almost as if peanut butter was made for cookies—the sweet/salty connection, the fat substitute, the starchiness that blends well with flour. So here's a set of American favorites: peanut butter and jelly thumbprints, peanut butter snickerdoodles, and peanut butter bar cookies. And here are some decidedly American takes on international favorites: macaroons, biscotti, and even rugalach. In other words, get out the baking sheets— because peanut butter is about to take over your kitchen!

PB&J THUMBPRINT COOKIES

These are old-fashioned cookies from your grandmother's era, but sure to cure the PB&J cravings of the most die-hard fans. You make a rich buttery dough, bake it halfway, press a dent in the center of each cookie, and fill it with jam that melts as it continues to bake.

MAKES ABOUT 24 COOKIES

1 stick (8 tablespoons) cool unsalted butter, cut into chunks

6 tablespoons creamy standard peanut butter

⅓ cup packed light brown sugar

¼ cup granulated sugar

2 large egg yolks, at room temperature

2 teaspoons vanilla extract

1 cup all-purpose flour

¼ teaspoon salt, optional

2 large egg whites, lightly beaten in a small bowl

1½ cups finely ground, roasted unsalted peanuts, placed on a large plate

½ cup Concord grape jelly

1. Position the rack in the center of the oven and preheat the oven to 375°F. Line a large baking sheet with a silicone baking mat or parchment paper; set it aside.

2. Beat the butter and peanut butter in a large bowl with an electric mixer at medium speed until light and creamy, about 1 minute. Add the brown sugar and granulated sugar; continue beating until light and pale brown, about 2 minutes, scraping down the sides of the bowl with a rubber spatula as necessary. Beat in the egg yolks and vanilla until smooth. Turn off the beaters; add the flour (and salt, if using). Beat at low speed just until the batter begins to cohere into a ball. Turn off and remove the beaters, scraping any excess batter back into the bowl; mix in any remaining flour with your hands, just until the batter is uniform in color if still a little grainy.

3. Pull off a small amount of dough, about the size of a walnut, and roll it into a ball between your palms. Dip it fully in the beaten egg whites, shake off any excess, then roll it in the ground peanuts. Place on the prepared baking sheet; flatten slightly with the palm of your hand. Continue making the cookies, spacing them about 2 inches apart.

4. Bake for 10 minutes, then take the tray out of the oven. Use the handle of a wooden spoon to make a small indentation in each cookie without pressing through to the baking sheet underneath. (You can use your thumb, but be careful because the cookies are hot.) Place 1 teaspoon jelly in each indentation. Return the baking sheet to the oven and continue baking until the cookies have dry, firm edges, are lightly browned, and the jelly has melted, about 10 more minutes. Cool the cookies on the baking sheet for 2 minutes, then transfer to a wire rack to cool completely. Use a second lined baking sheet for additional cookies, or cool this baking sheet for 5 minutes and replace the parchment paper if it's frizzled or singed. The cookies can be stored in an airtight container, between sheets of wax paper, for up to 3 days.

Customize Them!

Add 1 teaspoon ground cinnamon or ground ginger or ¼ teaspoon grated nutmeg with the flour.

Substitute chopped pecans or walnuts for the roasted unsalted peanuts.

Of course, you can use any jam or jelly you prefer: cherry, raspberry, strawberry, or red currant. However, we do not recommend using preserves or marmalades because the individual chunks of fruit may be too large to fit in the center of the cookies.

PEANUT BUTTER BAR COOKIES

These classic bar cookies may be a little retro, but they're as good as ever with peanut butter and oats—and no flour at all, so they're both crunchy and moist!

MAKES 24 BAR COOKIES

12 tablespoons (1½ sticks) cool unsalted butter, cut into chunks

¾ cup crunchy peanut butter

1¼ cups dark brown sugar

½ cup light corn syrup

2 teaspoons vanilla extract

4½ cups rolled oats (do not use steel-cut or quick-cooking oats)

12 ounces semisweet or bittersweet chocolate, chopped, or 1½ cups semisweet chocolate chips

¾ cup creamy standard peanut butter

1. Position the rack in the center of the oven and preheat the oven to 375°F.

2. Use an electric mixer to beat the butter, crunchy peanut butter, brown sugar, corn syrup, and vanilla in a large bowl until creamy and light, about 2 minutes, scraping down the sides of the bowl as necessary. Beat in the oats until fully incorporated. Spread this mixture into a 9 × 13-inch pan.

3. Bake until set and browned, about 30 minutes. Transfer the bar cookies in the pan to a wire rack and cool for 10 minutes.

4. Meanwhile, melt the chocolate in the top half of a double boiler set over about 1 inch of simmering water or in a medium bowl that fits securely over a medium saucepan with about the same amount of simmering water. Stir until half the chocolate has melted, then remove the top half of the double boiler or the bowl from the heat and continue stirring until all the chocolate has melted. Stir in the creamy peanut butter until smooth. (If for any reason the chocolate breaks into tight threads and a thin liquid, whisk in cream in 2-tablespoon increments until the chocolate is again glossy and smooth.) Set aside to cool for 5 minutes.

5. Unmold the bar cookies by placing a cutting board over the baking dish and turning the whole thing upside down. Tap a few times and the bar cookies will come out in one piece. Put a second cutting board over the cookies and invert again so that they are now right side up. Spread the melted chocolate mixture over the bar cookies, then place them on their cutting board in the refrigerator for 20 minutes to let the chocolate harden. Cut into 24 cookies; store them at room temperature in an airtight container for up to 4 days.

Customize Them!

Mix ½ cup of any of the following into the chocolate with the creamy peanut butter: chopped dried figs, chopped pecans, chopped roasted unsalted peanuts, chopped walnuts, dried cranberries, M&M Baking Bits, raisins, or Reese's Pieces.

PEANUT BUTTER BISCOTTI

These twice-baked hard Italian cookies are given the good ol' American razzmatazz with peanut butter. They're perfect for dunking in coffee, milk, or red wine.

MAKES ABOUT 36 BISCOTTI

1½ cups plus 2 tablespoons all-purpose flour, plus additional for dusting your work surface

½ teaspoon ground cinnamon

½ teaspoon baking powder

½ teaspoon baking soda

¼ teaspoon salt, optional

¾ cup sugar

¾ cup crunchy standard peanut butter

2 large eggs plus 1 large egg yolk, at room temperature

1. Position two baking racks in the upper and lower thirds of the oven and preheat the oven to 350°F. Line a large, lipped baking sheet with a silicone baking mat or parchment paper; set aside. Whisk the flour, cinnamon, baking powder, baking soda, and salt, if using, in a medium bowl until uniform; set aside as well.

2. In a large bowl, whisk the sugar, peanut butter, eggs, and egg yolk until smooth. Stir in the prepared flour mixture with a wooden spoon until a dough forms. Gather it together in the bowl, then dust a clean work surface with flour and turn the dough out onto it. Shape the dough into a mound, then divide it in half. Lightly flour each half, then use your palms to roll them into logs about 10 inches long and 1½ inches in diameter. Place both logs on the baking sheet, spacing them about 3 inches apart.

3. Bake in the upper third of the oven for 30 minutes, until somewhat dried out. Remove the baking sheet and cool the logs at room temperature for 10 minutes. Reduce the oven temperature to 275°F.

4. Transfer the logs to a cutting board and slice them with a serrated knife into ½-inch-wide cookies. Slicing on the diagonal will produce longer cookies. Lay the cookies on two large baking sheets, spacing them about 1 inch apart. Bake in the top and bottom thirds of the oven for 20 minutes. Remove the baking sheets and turn each cookie over. Reverse the sheets top to bottom and continue baking until the cookies are hard, about 20 more minutes. Cool on the sheets for 5 minutes, then transfer to a wire rack to cool completely. The biscotti can be stored in an airtight container at room temperature for up to 2 weeks.

Customize Them!

Substitute ¼ teaspoon grated nutmeg for the cinnamon.

Stir in ¾ cup mini chocolate chips with the cinnamon.

Stir in ⅔ cup dried cherries, dried cranberries, or dried currants with the cinnamon, but first chop the cherries or cranberries until they are the size of currants.

Add 1 tablespoon vanilla extract, 2 teaspoons maple extract, or 1½ teaspoons rum extract with the eggs.

PEANUT BUTTER CHOCOLATE CHIP COOKIES

Since peanut butter itself is starchy, we find the most tender chocolate chip cookies are made with a combination of all-purpose flour and whole wheat pastry flour, a higher starch, more finely ground flour made from a soft wheat with the germ ground into the mix. You can find it at most gourmet markets or from outlets listed in the Source Guide (page 237).

MAKES ABOUT 40 COOKIES

1½ cups semisweet chocolate chips (about 12 ounces)

1 cup all-purpose flour

½ cup whole wheat or whole-grain pastry flour

1 teaspoon baking soda

½ teaspoon salt, optional

1 cup chunky standard peanut butter

¼ cup solid vegetable shortening

½ cup packed dark brown sugar

¼ cup granulated sugar

¼ cup honey (see page 10)

2 large eggs, at room temperature

2 teaspoons vanilla extract

1. Position the racks in the top and bottom thirds of the oven; preheat the oven to 350°F. Whisk the chocolate chips, all-purpose flour, pastry flour, baking soda, and salt, if using, in a medium bowl until well combined; set aside.

2. In a large bowl, beat the chunky peanut butter and vegetable shortening with an electric mixer at medium speed until light and airy, about 1 minute. Beat in the brown sugar, granulated sugar, and honey until the mixture's color lightens a little, about 1 more minute. Scrape down the sides of the bowl with a rubber spatula, and beat in the eggs, one at a time, then beat in the vanilla. Turn off the beaters, add the flour mixture, and beat at a very low speed just until combined if still grainy.

3. Gather up a rounded tablespoon of the dough and roll it into a ball in your hand. Place it on an ungreased, nonstick baking sheet. Continue making the balls until you have filled two baking sheets, spacing the balls about 3 inches apart (see Note). Flatten them slightly with your fingers, just until they look like partially deflated basketballs but not until they crack at the sides.

4. Bake for 7 minutes, then switch the baking sheets top to bottom and front to back. Continue baking until browned and dry to the touch, if still a little soft, about 7 more minutes. Cool on the baking sheets for 2 minutes, then transfer to a wire rack to cool completely. Cool the baking sheet for 5 minutes before making additional batches. Store the cookies at room temperature in an airtight container for up to 3 days; or place them in zip-closed plastic bags and freeze them for up to 3 months.

NOTE: *If you have only one baking sheet, bake the cookies for 6 minutes in the upper third of the oven, then switch them to the lower third and continue baking as directed.*

Customize Them!

For crunchier cookies, replace the 2 large eggs with 1 large egg and 2 large egg whites.

For chewier cookies, reduce the granulated sugar to 2 tablespoons and add 2 tablespoons light corn syrup with it.

Reduce the semisweet chocolate chips to ¾ cup; add ¾ cup peanut butter chips with the remaining semisweet chips.

Reduce the semisweet chocolate chips to ¾ cup; add ¾ cup white chocolate chips with the remaining semisweet chips.

Reduce the vanilla extract to 1 teaspoon; add 1 teaspoon banana or rum flavoring with the remaining vanilla extract.

PEANUT BUTTER COOKIES

Look no further for the ultimate peanut butter cookie: unadorned, straightforward, and tasty. They're cakey and not too sweet, perfect with a cup of coffee or tea.

MAKES ABOUT 42 COOKIES

2½ cups all-purpose flour

2 teaspoons baking powder

½ teaspoon salt, optional

1 cup sugar

½ cup plus 2 tablespoons creamy standard peanut butter

¼ cup solid vegetable shortening

⅔ cup canola oil

2 large eggs, at room temperature

1 tablespoon vanilla extract

1. Position the rack in the center of the oven; preheat the oven to 350°F. Whisk the flour, baking powder, and salt, if using, in a medium bowl; set aside.

2. Use an electric mixer at medium speed to beat the sugar, peanut butter, and shortening in a large bowl until creamy and smooth, about 2 minutes. Beat in the oil, then the eggs, one at a time. Scrape down the sides of the bowl and beat in the vanilla until smooth.

3. Remove the beaters (scrape any excess back into the batter) and stir in the prepared flour mixture with a wooden spoon, just until the batter coheres into a mass and can be gathered into a ball. Scoop out the dough in 1-tablespoon increments and roll them into balls about the size of a whole walnut. Place the balls on a large ungreased baking sheet, spacing them about 2 inches apart. Use a fork to press a crosshatch pattern into the cookies, pressing down one direction with the tines, then rotating them 90 degrees and pressing down a second time. Don't press the ball completely flat so that the sides crack open; it should look like a mostly flattened basketball with tire marks running both ways across it.

4. Bake until firm and light to the touch, about 18 minutes. Cool on the baking sheet for 2 minutes, then transfer the cookies to a wire rack and cool completely. The cookies can be stored in an airtight container at room temperature for up to 1 week. They can also be frozen for up to 4 months; let them stand for 15 minutes at room temperature before serving.

Customize Them!

Stir ⅔ cup of any of the following or any combination of the following into the flour mixture before it's added to the wet ingredients: butterscotch chips, chocolate-covered espresso beans, chopped dried bananas, chopped pecans, chopped roasted unsalted peanuts, chopped walnuts, dried raspberries, M&M Baking Bits, peanut butter chips, raisins, Reese's Pieces, semisweet chocolate chips, or white chocolate chips.

PEANUT BUTTER CREAM SANDWICH COOKIES

Here are the classic standards: cream sandwich cookies made from two crisp peanut butter rounds and a decadently smooth peanut butter filling.

MAKES 30 SANDWICH COOKIES

FOR THE COOKIES

1¾ cup all-purpose flour

½ teaspoon baking soda

¼ teaspoon salt, optional

1 cup sugar

¾ cup solid vegetable shortening

¾ cup creamy natural peanut butter

¼ cup dark corn syrup

1 large egg yolk, at room temperature

2 teaspoons vanilla extract

FOR THE CREAM FILLING

⅔ cup creamy standard peanut butter

¼ cup solid vegetable shortening

1¼ cups confectioners' sugar

2 teaspoons vanilla extract

1. Position the rack in the center of the oven and preheat the oven to 350°F. Whisk the flour, baking soda, and salt, if using, in a medium bowl until the baking soda is evenly distributed; set aside.

2. Beat the sugar, shortening, and natural peanut butter in a large bowl with an electric mixer at medium speed until creamy and soft, about 2 minutes. Scrape down the sides of the bowl with a rubber spatula, beat in the corn syrup, then beat in the egg yolk and vanilla until smooth. Turn off the beaters, add the prepared flour mixture, and beat at a very low speed until a dough gathers together in the bowl.

3. Dot your work surface with water and lay a large piece of wax paper on the water droplets (the water will keep it from skidding around while you roll out the dough). Divide the dough into thirds and place one-third on the wax paper. Press into a squat circle and cover with a second large sheet of wax paper. Roll out the dough until it is ¼ inch, then cut out cookies using a 1½-inch round cookie cutter. Place these on a large ungreased baking sheet about 2 inches apart.

4. Bake until set but soft, about 12 minutes. Let the cookies cool on the baking sheet for 2 minutes, then transfer them to a wire rack to cool completely. Cool the sheet at least 5 minutes before using it again.

5. Roll out a second piece of the dough as indicated in step 3 and bake as directed in step 4. Then repeat with the last piece of dough.

6. Once the cookies are completely cooled, make the cream filling by beating the standard peanut butter and shortening in a large bowl with an electric mixer at medium speed until creamy. Beat in the confectioners' sugar and vanilla until a smooth icing forms. Place a scant 2 teaspoons of the filling on the flat bottom of one of the cookies and sandwich it between another cookie, flat bottom to flat bottom. Continue making all the filled sandwich cookies. They can be stored in an airtight container at room temperature for up to 5 days.

Customize It!

Add 1 teaspoon ground cinnamon, ¼ teaspoon grated nutmeg, ¼ teaspoon ground allspice, ¼ teaspoon grated mace, and/or ⅛ teaspoon ground cloves with the baking soda.

    Substitute chocolate, maple, orange, or rum extracts for the vanilla extract in the filling.

PEANUT BUTTER GINGERBREAD COOKIES

Don't feel constrained by the round cookie cutter we recommend for these spicy, chewy cookies—use any shape you wish.

MAKES ABOUT 60 COOKIES

Nonstick spray or unsalted butter for greasing the baking sheets

2 cups all-purpose flour, plus additional for dusting

2 teaspoons ground ginger

1½ teaspoons ground cinnamon

1 teaspoon baking soda

¼ teaspoon salt, optional

6 tablespoons cool unsalted butter, cut into chunks

6 tablespoons creamy standard peanut butter

½ cup sugar

½ cup molasses, preferably unsulphured molasses (see page 13)

1 large egg white, at room temperature

1. Position the racks in the top and bottom thirds of the oven; preheat it to 350°F. Lightly spray or butter a large baking sheet; set aside. Whisk the flour, ginger, cinnamon, baking soda, and salt, if using, in a medium bowl until the spices are well distributed in the mixture; set aside.

2. Beat the butter and peanut butter in a large bowl with an electric mixer at medium speed until light and fluffy, about 2 minutes. Beat in the sugar until fairly creamy, about 1 more minute. Scrape down the sides of the bowl with a rubber spatula, then beat in the molasses until smooth. Finally, beat in the egg white until uniform. Turn off the beaters, add the flour mixture, and beat at low speed just until the dough begins to gather together and the flour has dissolved.

3. Dust your work surface with flour. Divide the dough in half and place one-half on your work surface. Dust it and a rolling pin with flour. Roll the dough to a large circle about ¼ inch thick; use additional flour as necessary to keep the dough from sticking. Use a 2-inch-round cookie cutter to cut out as many cookies as possible; use a thin metal spatula to transfer them to the prepared baking sheet, spacing them about 1 inch apart.

4. Bake until slightly dry and a little firm but not hard, about 7 minutes. Cool the cookies on the baking sheet for 2 minutes, then transfer to a wire rack to cool completely. Lightly spray or butter a second baking sheet and continue making cookies, or cool this first cookie sheet for 5 minutes before respraying it or buttering it lightly again and baking more cookies. The cookies can be stored in an airtight container at room temperature for up to 5 days, or they can be frozen in an airtight container between sheets of wax paper for up to 3 months.

Peanut Butter Gingerbread Men, Anyone?

After rolling the dough out, use a gingerbread man–shaped cookie cutter to cut out as many cookies as possible and bake them for a total of about 9 minutes, or until slightly dry and a little firm without being hard. Once the cookies have cooled to room temperature on a wire rack, frost them with Chocolate Icing (below).

CHOCOLATE ICING

MAKES A LITTLE MORE THAN ½ CUP

3 tablespoons cocoa powder

2 tablespoons unsalted butter, at room temperature

1½ tablespoons half-and-half or heavy cream

2 teaspoons light corn syrup

¾ cup confectioners' sugar, maybe a little less or more

Beat the butter, cocoa powder, half-and-half, and corn syrup in a medium bowl with a mixer at medium speed until thick and creamy, about 4 minutes. Then beat in the confectioners' sugar in 2-tablespoon increments until a thick icing forms. Spread this onto the cooled cookies with a small rubber spatula or an icing spatula.

If desired, decorate the gingerbread men with red hots and raisins for their eyes, nose, and buttons.

PEANUT BUTTER MACAROONS

These are the classic French cookies, little puffed-up dots of batter, served in the middle of the day or after dinner with a cup of espresso. The recipe makes plenty—although each is just a bite.

MAKES 110–120 MACAROONS

One 16-ounce jar creamy natural peanut butter, any oil that's separated from it drained off and discarded

2 cups sugar

6 large egg whites, at room temperature

1. Position the rack in the center of the oven and preheat the oven to 375°F. Cover a large baking sheet with parchment paper or a silicone baking mat; set aside.

2. Beat the peanut butter and sugar in a large bowl with an electric mixer at medium speed until very smooth, about 5 minutes. You want most of the sugar to dissolve into the peanut butter. Scrape down the sides of the bowl as necessary while the mixture beats.

3. Place the egg whites in a second bowl. With the mixer running at medium speed, add them to the peanut butter mixture in 1-tablespoon increments. Once all the egg whites have been added, continue beating until the mixture is smooth, thick, and pastelike. (This may take up to 5 minutes.) Scoop this mixture into a pastry bag fitted with a ½-inch tip; or cut a small hole in one corner of a zip-closed plastic bag, fit it with a ½-inch tip, add the dough, and squeeze it down to the tip. Squeeze out 1-inch rounds onto the prepared baking sheet, spacing them about 1 inch apart and swirling the mixture up into a little cowlick as you finish each one. Alternatively, you can drop the batter by teaspoons onto the sheet, making little irregular mounds.

4. Bake until dry and set, about 11 minutes. Cool them on the baking sheet for 5 minutes before transferring them with a metal spatula to a wire rack to cool completely. They will firm up as they cool. Cool the baking sheet 5 more minutes before adding more rounds; if you've used parchment paper, replace it before a second baking. Store the macaroons at room temperature in an airtight container or a plastic bag for up to 5 days.

PEANUT BUTTER MACAROON SANDWICH COOKIES

MAKES 55-60 MACAROONS

1 recipe Peanut Butter Macaroons (page 158)

The classic macaroons are actually sandwich cookies. Spread about ½ teaspoon raspberry or strawberry jam on the bottom of one of the macaroons, then sandwich another to it, bottom to bottom. Place it on a wire rack and continue making the cookies until you've sandwiched them all with the jam (you'll need about ½ cup plus 2 tablespoons jam).

Or make chocolate sandwiched macaroons by placing 3 ounces chopped semisweet chocolate in the top half of a double boiler set over a pot with about 1 inch of simmering water or in a medium bowl that fits securely over a medium saucepan with about the same amount of simmering water. Stir until half the chocolate has melted, then remove the top half of the double boiler or the bowl from the heat and continue stirring until all the chocolate has melted. Cool for 5 minutes. Smear 1 teaspoon of the melted chocolate on the flat bottom of one of the cookies, then press a second cookie's flat bottom against the chocolate, thereby making a small sandwich cookie. Place the filled cookies on a wire rack to allow the chocolate to firm up at room temperature, about 1 hour. Repeat with the remaining cookies and chocolate.

PEANUT BUTTER OAT COOKIES

If you like crunchy cookies, leave these classic oat cookies in the oven for another minute or so, just until they're firm to the touch.

MAKES ABOUT 50 COOKIES

1½ cups all-purpose flour

1¼ cups rolled oats (do not use steel-cut or quick-cooking oats)

1½ teaspoons baking soda

½ teaspoon salt, optional

1 cup chunky standard peanut butter

8 tablespoons (1 stick) cool unsalted butter, cut into chunks

¼ cup solid vegetable shortening

¼ cup light corn syrup

¾ cup packed dark brown sugar

½ cup granulated sugar

2 large eggs, at room temperature

2 teaspoons vanilla extract

1. Position the rack in the middle of the oven; preheat the oven to 350°F. Whisk the flour, oats, baking soda, and salt, if using, in a medium bowl; set aside.

2. Beat the peanut butter, butter, and vegetable shortening in a large bowl with an electric mixer at medium speed until light and fluffy, about 2 minutes. Beat in the corn syrup, then scrape down the sides of the bowl, and add both kinds of sugar. Continue beating at medium speed until the sugar dissolves and the color of the batter lightens somewhat, about 2 minutes. Beat in the eggs, one at a time, then the vanilla.

3. Turn off the mixer and add the flour mixture all at once. Beat at a very low speed, just until the flour has been thoroughly moistened. Do not overbeat. Drop by tablespoonfuls onto a large, nonstick baking sheet, spacing the mounds about 3 inches apart.

4. Bake until golden, a little puffed, and dry to the touch if still soft, about 13 minutes. Cool on the baking sheet for 2 minutes, then transfer the cookies to a wire rack to cool completely. Use a second baking sheet for another batch, or let this baking sheet cool for 5 minutes before dropping more batter mounds on it. Store the cookies at room temperature in an airtight container for up to 3 days, or place them in a zip-closed plastic bag and freeze them for up to 3 months.

Customize Them!

Add 1 teaspoon ground cinnamon, ½ teaspoon finely minced dried orange peel, or 1 teaspoon grated nutmeg with the baking soda.

Add 1 cup of any of the following with the dry ingredients: chopped dried bananas, chopped dried figs, chopped dried strawberries, chopped Heath bars, chopped pecans, chopped pitted dates, chopped roasted unsalted peanuts, chopped walnuts, dried cherries, dried cranberries, M&M Baking Bits, mini chocolate chips, raisins, or Reese's Pieces.

Substitute banana, maple, orange, or rum extracts for the vanilla.

PEANUT BUTTER REFRIGERATOR COOKIES

Refrigerator cookies may be the easiest of all—you make the dough in advance, roll it into a log, and store it in your refrigerator for up to 2 weeks, slicing off as many cookies as you'd like to bake at any one time. Better yet, you can freeze those logs, tightly sealed with plastic wrap, for up to 2 months; let them thaw in the refrigerator for 4 hours.

MAKES ABOUT 80 COOKIES

2¼ cups all-purpose flour, plus additional for dusting your work surface

1 cup whole wheat or whole-grain pastry flour (see headnote page 149)

1 teaspoon baking soda

½ teaspoon salt, optional

16 tablespoons (2 sticks) cool, unsalted butter, cut into small pieces

1 cup chunky standard peanut butter

¾ cup packed dark brown sugar

⅔ cup granulated sugar

2 large eggs, at room temperature

2 teaspoons vanilla extract

1. Whisk the flour, whole wheat pastry flour, baking soda, and salt, if using, in a medium bowl; set aside.

2. Beat the butter and peanut butter in a large bowl with an electric mixer at medium speed until airy and light, about 2 minutes. Add both sugars and continue beating at medium speed until you can't feel any sugar granules if you rub a small dab between your fingers, about 2 minutes. Scrape down the sides of the bowl with a rubber spatula and beat in the eggs, one at a time, then the vanilla.

3. Turn off the beaters and add the flour mixture. Beat at very low speed just until a soft, pliable dough forms and there is no more dry flour visible. Scrape down the beaters, remove them, and gather the dough into a large, loose ball in the bowl. Lightly dust a clean work surface with flour and turn the dough out onto it. Divide the ball in half and use your palms to roll them into logs about 10 inches long. Don't press down; just roll it gently back and forth on the work surface.

4. Wrap each log tightly in plastic wrap and chill in the refrigerator for at least 4 hours, or store them there for up to 2 weeks. To help the logs better keep their shape, cut the inner cardboard tube of a paper towel roll in half the long way, so that you make two long, semicircular containers that will cup the wrapped logs as they rest in the refrigerator.

5. To bake the cookies, position the rack in the center of the oven and preheat the oven to 350°F. Unwrap one of the logs and slice off as many ¼-inch-thick round disks as you desire. Place these on a large nonstick baking sheet, spacing them about 1 inch apart. Wrap the remainder of the log in plastic wrap and return it to the refrigerator. Bake until golden and slightly dry to the touch, if still soft, about 15 minutes. Cool on the baking sheet for 2 minutes, then transfer the cookies to a wire rack to cool completely. They can be stored at room temperature in an airtight container for up to 4 days.

MAKING SANDWICH COOKIES

Refrigerator cookies make easy sandwich cookies. Consider spreading any of the following on half the cookies (1 and 2 teaspoons as the filling on each, depending on your preference) and sandwiching those cookies with the other half: grape jam, Marshmallow Fluff or Marshmallow Crème, raspberry jam, or strawberry jam. Or use this chocolate frosting.

EASY CHOCOLATE FROSTING

MAKES ABOUT 1¼ CUPS

2 ounces unsweetened chocolate, chopped
¼ cup water

2 tablespoons light corn syrup

¼ teaspoon salt

½ teaspoon vanilla extract

2½ cups confectioners' sugar

Place the chocolate in a medium bowl and set aside. Stir the water, corn syrup, and salt in a small saucepan until the corn syrup dissolves, then set the pan over medium heat. Do not stir, but the moment the mixture comes to a simmer, remove the pan from the heat.

Pour the hot syrup over the chopped chocolate, stirring until the chocolate has melted. Add the confectioners' sugar and vanilla; stir until incorporated. Cool for 5 minutes, then use this frosting as a filling for the cookies.

PEANUT BUTTER RUGALACH

Rugalach has always been a favorite in Jewish delis, but these little rolled, filled, pastry-style cookies were never made with peanut butter—until now.

MAKES 32 RUGALACH

1½ cups all-purpose flour, plus additional for dusting

1¼ cups cake flour

¼ teaspoon salt

16 tablespoons (2 sticks) cool, unsalted butter, cut into chunks

8 ounces cream cheese (regular or low-fat but not nonfat), softened to room temperature

¼ cup granulated sugar

1 large egg plus 1 large egg white, at room temperature

4 teaspoons vanilla extract

1 cup creamy standard peanut butter

⅓ cup packed light brown sugar

3 tablespoons milk (regular, low-fat, or nonfat)

½ teaspoon ground cinnamon

1. Whisk both flours and salt in a medium bowl; set aside.

2. Beat the butter and cream cheese in a large bowl with an electric mixer at medium speed until soft and creamy, about 2 minutes. Add the granulated sugar and continue beating until dissolved, about 2 more minutes. Beat in 1 whole egg, then 2 teaspoons of the vanilla.

3. Turn off the beaters and add half the flour mixture. Beat on low until incorporated, then add the remainder of the flour mixture and continue beating on low until a soft dough forms. Turn off the beaters, scrape them down, and gather the dough into a ball in the bowl. Cover the bowl with plastic wrap and chill it in the refrigerator for at least 4 hours but not more than 12 hours.

4. Position the rack in the center of the oven and preheat the oven to 400°F.

5. Make the filling by beating the peanut butter, light brown sugar, milk, cinnamon, the remaining egg white, and the remaining 2 teaspoons vanilla in a medium bowl until fairly smooth and creamy. Set aside at room temperature.

6. Lightly dust a clean work surface with flour. Divide the flour dough in half; gather one-half into a ball. Place it on the prepared work surface and very lightly dust the dough with flour. Press it lightly with your hands into a small circle, then roll it into a circle about 12 inches in diameter. Spread half the peanut butter filling over the dough, leaving a ¼-inch border around the circumference. Cut the circle into 16, even, pie-shaped wedges, starting at the center point and moving out to the circumference for each cut. (You can also do this with a large knife, one large enough to measure the diameter of the circle—keep rotating the knife on the circle's diameter until you've made 16 wedges.)

7. Separate these wedges from each other a little, then roll each one up, starting at the wider, outside edge and rolling toward the tip. Some of the filling will ooze out a little, creating what looks like a second strip of darker dough along the edge of the lighter dough. Place the rolled cookies tip side down on a large, lipped baking sheet, preferably a nonstick sheet, spacing them about 1 inch apart. Repeat this whole process with the second half of the dough, making 16 more rugalach.

8. Bake until lightly browned and somewhat firm to the touch, 18 to 20 minutes. Cool on the baking sheet for 2 minutes, then transfer to a wire rack to cool completely. The rugalach can be stored in an airtight container at room temperature for up to 4 days. They can also be frozen in an airtight container for up to 3 months; let them thaw on a wire rack at room temperature for at least 15 minutes before serving.

PEANUT BUTTER SNICKERDOODLES

Here's an American classic at its best: a homegrown sugar cookie that's been reimagined with peanut butter. These cookies are a little softer than the originals; we think the texture better matches all that creamy peanut butter.

MAKES ABOUT 36 COOKIES

2 cups all-purpose flour

2 teaspoons cream of tartar

1 teaspoon baking soda

½ teaspoon salt, optional

¾ cup creamy standard peanut butter

½ cup solid vegetable shortening

2 cups sugar

2 large eggs, at room temperature

1 tablespoon vanilla extract

2 teaspoons ground cinnamon

1. Whisk the flour, cream of tartar, baking soda, and salt, if using, in a medium bowl; set aside.

2. Beat the peanut butter and shortening in a large bowl with an electric mixer at medium speed until creamy and light, about 1 minute. Add 1¾ cups sugar and continue beating until the color of the mixture lightens. Scrape down the sides of the bowl with a rubber spatula, then beat in the eggs, one at a time. Beat in the vanilla. Turn off the mixer and add the flour mixture all at once. Beat at a low speed, just until a smooth dough comes together. Do not overbeat. Remove the mixer, after first scraping down the blades, and set the dough aside for 10 minutes.

3. Position the rack in the center of the oven and preheat the oven to 350°F. Line a lipped baking sheet with a silicon baking mat or parchment paper; set aside. Mix the remaining ¼ cup sugar and cinnamon in a small bowl.

4. Gather up a rounded tablespoon of the dough and gently firm it into a ball in your hand. Roll it in the sugar mixture, then place it on the prepared baking sheet. Continue making balls and rolling them in the sugar mixture until you have filled the sheet, spacing the balls 3 inches apart.

5. Bake until lightly browned, crackled, and flattened but still a little puffy, 13 to 15 minutes. Cool on the baking sheet for 2 minutes, then transfer to a wire rack to cool completely. While the cookies are baking, you can roll additional balls and coat them in sugar—to bake them, use a second lined baking sheet or allow the one that's been in the oven to cool for 5 minutes. If you've used parchment paper, replace it before you bake a second batch. When cooled, store the cookies in an airtight container for up to 4 days; or seal them in zip-closed plastic bags and freeze them for up to 3 months.

Customize Them!

Substitute banana, maple, orange, or rum extracts for the vanilla extract.

Desserts

Consider this set of rich desserts our guarantee that you can still bring out the kid in everyone with the likes of Peanut Butter Bread Pudding, Peanut Butter Semifreddo, Peanut Butter Torte. We've got sheet cakes, blondies, and brownies, too—because sometimes, we still crave the classics (when we're not craving peanut butter).

APPLE COBBLER WITH A PEANUT BUTTER CRUNCH TOPPING

What's the best part of a cobbler—the sweet fruit filling or the crunchy topping? You don't have to choose with this easy dessert that takes full advantage of the spectacular combination of apples and peanut butter. One warning: have lots of vanilla ice cream on hand.

MAKES SIX SERVINGS

7 medium tart apples, such as Granny Smith or McIntosh, peeled, cored, and thinly sliced (about 6 cups)

⅓ cup plus 2 tablespoons granulated sugar

¼ cup all-purpose flour

1 tablespoon lemon juice

1 tablespoon quick-cooking tapioca

1 teaspoon ground cinnamon

6 tablespoons rolled oats (do not use steel-cut or quick-cooking oats)

¼ cup crunchy standard peanut butter

¼ cup packed dark brown sugar

3 tablespoons unsalted butter, at room temperature, plus additional for greasing the pan

½ teaspoon vanilla extract

¼ teaspoon salt, optional

1. Position the rack in the center of the oven and preheat the oven to 375°F. Lightly butter an 8-inch baking dish; set aside.

2. Mix the apple slices, ⅓ cup granulated sugar, 2 tablespoons flour, lemon juice, tapioca, and ½ teaspoon cinnamon in a large bowl until the apple slices are thoroughly coated with the sugary mixture. Pour this mixture into the prepared pan, spreading it evenly to the corners.

3. Use a fork to mix the oats, peanut butter, brown sugar, butter, vanilla, the remaining 2 tablespoons granulated sugar, the remaining 2 tablespoons flour, the remaining ½ teaspoon cinnamon, and the salt, if using, in a medium bowl until the consistency of a crumbly muffin topping. Sprinkle this mixture evenly over the apple mixture in the pan.

4. Bake until the apple filling is bubbling and the top is lightly browned, about 45 minutes. Cool on a wire rack at least 5 minutes before serving. After the cobbler has completely cooled, it can be stored, tightly covered, in the refrigerator for up to 4 days.

More cobblers!

To make a blueberry cobbler, use 6 cups fresh blueberries in the filling.

To make a peach cobbler, use 6 cups fresh, sliced peaches or 6 cups still-frozen peach slices in the filling; increase the quick-cooking tapioca to 2 tablespoons.

To make a pear cobbler, use about 8 ripe pears, peeled, cored, and sliced (yielding about 6 cups of slices); increase the quick-cooking tapioca to 2 tablespoons.

To make a raspberry cobbler, use 5 cups of fresh or frozen (do not thaw) raspberries in the filling; increase the sugar in the filling to ½ cup.

To make a strawberry rhubarb cobbler, use 3 cups sliced fresh strawberries and 3 cups fresh or frozen (do not thaw) sliced rhubarb; increase the sugar in the filling to ⅔ cup and increase the quick-cooking tapioca to 2 tablespoons.

CHOCOLATE CUPCAKES WITH PEANUT BUTTER CENTERS

I f you like chocolate peanut butter candies, you may have found your grail: moist, delicate cupcakes with a dense peanut butter center.

MAKES 12 CUPCAKES

12 paper muffin cups

1 cup all-purpose flour

⅓ cup cocoa powder, preferably natural cocoa powder (see page 8)

½ teaspoon baking soda

⅛ teaspoon salt

¾ cup plus 3 tablespoons sugar

6 tablespoons cool unsalted butter, cut into chunks

2 large eggs, at room temperature

2 teaspoons vanilla extract

½ cup milk (regular, low-fat, or nonfat)

½ cup creamy standard peanut butter

1. Position the rack in the center of the oven; preheat the oven to 350°F. Line a 12-indentation or two 6-indentation cupcake or muffin tins with 12 paper liners; set aside. Whisk the flour, cocoa powder, baking soda, and salt in a medium bowl until uniformly colored; set aside.

2. Beat ¾ cup sugar and the butter in a large bowl with an electric mixer at medium speed until light and fluffy, about 2 minutes. Beat in 1 whole egg, then 1 egg yolk (reserve the second white for later in the recipe), and the vanilla. Scrape down the sides of the bowl with a rubber spatula, then beat in ¼ cup milk until smooth. Beat in about half the flour mixture at a very low speed, then beat in the remainder of the milk, followed by the remainder of the flour mixture. Do not beat more than 20 seconds or so after you add this last bit of flour or the cupcakes may turn tough. Fill the prepared indentations halfway full with the batter; set the remainder of the batter aside.

3. Clean and dry the beaters, then beat the peanut butter, the remaining egg white, and the remaining 3 tablespoons sugar in a small bowl until creamy and light. Roll rounded tablespoons of this mixture into loose but nonetheless cohesive balls and press each into the batter in the tin. Don't press down until the ball touches the tin's bottom; rather, make sure the ball is about two-thirds covered with the batter. Use the remaining batter to cover the balls and fill the tins, spreading it as necessary with a rubber spatula.

4. Bake until puffed and dry if still soft to the touch, about 25 minutes. Cool in the pan for 10 minutes, then gently rock the cupcakes back and forth to loosen them from the indentations and transfer to a wire rack to cool completely. They can be stored in an airtight container at room temperature for up to 3 days. They can also be frozen in an airtight container or a large zip-closed bag for up to 3 months; let them come back to room temperature on a wire rack.

Customize It!

Stir in ½ cup cocoa nibs, chopped pecans, chopped roasted unsalted peanuts, or chopped walnuts with the flour.

Substitute 1 teaspoon maple or rum extract for the vanilla.

CHOCOLATE PEANUT BUTTER SHEET CAKE WITH A MARSHMALLOW PEANUT BUTTER FROSTING

Sheet cakes are great for parties, family reunions, or potlucks. You make a large, thin cake in a jelly-roll pan, then frost it without unmolding it—here, with a yummy peanut butter frosting made with Marshmallow Fluff.

MAKES 32 SERVINGS

FOR THE CHOCOLATE PEANUT BUTTER SHEET CAKE

2 cups sugar

1½ cups all-purpose flour, plus additional for dusting the pan

⅓ cup cocoa powder, preferably natural cocoa powder (see page 8)

2 teaspoons ground cinnamon

1 teaspoon baking soda

½ teaspoon salt

¾ cup creamy standard peanut butter

2 large eggs, at room temperature

1½ cups buttermilk (regular or low-fat but not nonfat)

12 tablespoons (1½ sticks) unsalted butter, melted and cooled, plus additional for greasing the pan

2 teaspoons vanilla extract

FOR THE MARSHMALLOW PEANUT BUTTER FROSTING

¾ cup creamy standard peanut butter

1 cup Marshmallow Fluff or Marshmallow Crème (see page 10)

¼ cup milk, preferably low-fat or nonfat

3 to 4 cups confectioners' sugar

1. After positioning the rack in the center of the oven, preheat the oven to 350°F. Lightly butter a 13 × 17-inch jelly-roll pan on the bottom and sides; add a little flour and tilt the pan around until it has a fine dusting of flour evenly across the bottom and sides; discard any excess flour. Set the pan aside.

2. Whisk the sugar, flour, cocoa powder, cinnamon, baking soda, and salt in a medium bowl; set aside.

3. Use an electric mixer to beat the peanut butter and eggs until creamy, about 1 minute. Add the buttermilk, melted butter, and vanilla; beat until smooth. Remove the beaters and stir in the prepared flour mixture with a wooden spoon until smooth but perhaps still a little grainy—there should be no white streaks of flour visible but overbeating will stretch and align the glutens and render the cake less tender. Pour this batter into the prepared jelly-roll pan.

4. Bake until a toothpick inserted in the center of the cake comes out with a few moist crumbs attached, about 30 minutes. Place the pan on a wire rack and cool completely, about 2 hours.

5. To make the frosting, use an electric mixer on medium speed to beat the peanut butter and Marshmallow Fluff in a large bowl until smooth, about 1 minute. Beat in the milk, then scrape down the sides of the bowl and beat in the confectioners' sugar in ⅓-cup increments until a smooth creamy frosting forms, one that can hold its shape when scooped onto a knife or icing spatula.

6. Place small dollops of the frosting all over the cake, then use an icing knife or an offset spatula to smooth the frosting evenly over the cake. Store at room temperature, lightly covered with plastic wrap, for up to 2 days. To keep the plastic wrap from sticking to the cake, you can insert several toothpicks into the cake and use them as tent poles to keep the plastic wrap off the frosting.

Customize It!

Add ¼ teaspoon grated allspice, mace, or nutmeg to the batter with the cinnamon.
Substitute banana, maple, or rum extracts for the vanilla in the cake batter.

Add ⅔ cup semisweet or bittersweet chocolate with the flour to the batter, or add ½ cup semisweet or bittersweet chocolate chips with the confectioners' sugar to the frosting, or do both!

Add ½ cup chopped Heath bars, cocoa nibs, M&M Baking Bits, Reese's Pieces, or toasted sweetened coconut to the frosting with the confectioners' sugar.

PEANUT BUTTER BLONDIES

We have a different recipe for these treats in *The Ultimate Brownie Book;* there, the focus is on the chocolate—just enough batter to hold the chips in place. Here, we've created a peanut butter lover's paradise: a moist but still dense blondie with just enough chocolate to set the intense peanut butter off.

MAKES 24 BLONDIES

1½ cups all-purpose flour

1 teaspoon baking powder

½ teaspoon salt, optional

1½ cups semisweet or bittersweet chocolate chips

8 tablespoons (1 stick) cool unsalted butter, cut into pieces, plus extra for greasing the pan

1 cup crunchy standard peanut butter

1 cup granulated sugar

¾ cup packed dark brown sugar

3 large eggs plus 1 large egg white, at room temperature

1 tablespoon vanilla extract

1. Position the rack in the center of the oven; preheat the oven to 350°F. Lightly grease a 9 × 13-inch baking pan with butter; set aside. Whisk the flour, baking powder, and salt, if using, in a medium bowl, then stir in the chocolate chips; set aside.

2. Beat the butter and peanut butter in a large bowl with an electric mixer at medium speed until light and fluffy, about 2 minutes. Add both sugars and continue beating at medium speed until they are dissolved in the batter and the color of the batter has lightened somewhat, about 2 minutes, scraping down the sides of the bowl as necessary with a rubber spatula. Beat in the eggs, one at a time, making sure each is thoroughly incorporated before adding the next. Beat in the egg white, then the vanilla.

3. Turn off the mixer and pour in the prepared flour mixture. Beat at very low speed, just until no flour is visible in the batter. The batter itself may still be grainy with flour, but there should be no lumps. Spread the batter into the prepared pan, taking care not to press down but using a rubber spatula to get it evenly to the pan's corners.

4. Bake until a toothpick inserted into the center of the cake comes out clean, about 35 minutes. Cool in the pan for 30 minutes. Place a large cutting board over the pan, flip it and the pan upside down, and rap the pan gently to release the blondie cake in one piece. Remove the pan, then place a wire rack over the blondies and flip the whole thing again, so the blondies are now top side up on the rack. Set aside to cool completely, about 20 minutes. Cut the blondies into 24 squares, making 6 cuts the short way and 4 the long way.

5. To store, wrap each blondie in a small piece of wax paper and place them in an airtight container for up to 4 days. You can also stack the wrapped blondies in an airtight container and freeze them for up to 3 months; let them stand at room temperature, still wrapped, for at least 20 minutes to thaw.

Customize It!

Mix in ⅔ cup of any of the following or any combination of the following into the batter after you've added the flour mixture: chopped banana chips, chopped honey-roasted peanuts, chopped pecans, chopped walnuts, cocoa nibs, dried blueberries, dried cranberries, mini marshmallows, and shredded sweetened coconut.

PEANUT BUTTER BREAD PUDDING

Everyone loves bread pudding. We actually prefer it with challah or egg bread—the bread itself is lighter and takes more readily to the custard as it bakes. You can use other yeast breads but leave them unwrapped on the counter overnight so they'll go stale and then won't turn to mush when soaked in the egg mixture.

MAKES ONE 9 × 13-INCH PAN OF BREAD PUDDING (ABOUT 10 SERVINGS)

Unsalted butter to grease the baking pan

4 cups milk, preferably low-fat or nonfat

6 large eggs, at room temperature

¾ cup creamy standard peanut butter

½ cup sugar

1 tablespoon vanilla extract

½ teaspoon salt, optional

½ cup raisins

6 cups cubed day-old egg bread, preferably challah or other egg bread

1. Position the rack in the center of the oven and preheat the oven to 350°F. Lightly butter a 9 × 13-inch baking pan and set it aside.

2. Put 1 cup milk, the eggs, peanut butter, sugar, vanilla, and salt, if using, in a large blender; blend until smooth, taking care that the peanut butter is thoroughly emulsified in the mixture. Pour into a large bowl, then whisk in the remaining 3 cups milk and the raisins. Stir in the bread, then set aside to soak for 10 minutes.

3. Pour this mixture into the prepared pan and bake until browned, puffed, and a little firm—a knife inserted into the middle of it should come out clean—about 45 minutes. Cool on a wire rack for at least 5 minutes before serving. Once completely cooled, the bread pudding can be stored, tightly covered, in the refrigerator for up to 3 days.

Customize It!

Substitute chopped dried bananas, chopped dried figs, dried blueberries, dried cranberries, or dried currants for the raisins.

Substitute ⅔ cup semisweet or bittersweet chocolate chips for the raisins.

Add ½ cup chopped roasted unsalted peanuts with the raisins.

Use any sweet "flavored" bread for the challah—hazelnut, raisin wheat, and so on.

PEANUT BUTTER BUNDT CAKE

This moist, sour cream–leavened cake is mined with a tunnel of peanut butter streusel. It's just the thing with an after-dinner cup of coffee and a game of hearts—or the next morning, for breakfast with the newspaper.

MAKES 12 SERVINGS

Nonstick spray

3 cups all-purpose flour

1½ teaspoons baking powder

1 teaspoon baking soda

½ teaspoon salt

⅓ cup packed dark brown sugar

2 tablespoons unsalted butter, melted and cooled

¾ cup chunky standard peanut butter

1 teaspoon ground cinnamon

1½ cups granulated sugar

12 tablespoons (1 stick plus 4 tablespoons) cool unsalted butter, cut into chunks

4 large eggs, at room temperature

1 cup sour cream (regular or low-fat—do not use nonfat)

2 teaspoons vanilla extract

1. Position the rack in the center of the oven; preheat the oven to 350°F. Lightly spray a 12-cup nonstick Bundt pan with nonstick spray; set aside. Whisk the flour, baking powder, baking soda, and salt in a medium bowl until well combined; set aside.

2. To prepare the streusel filling, mix the dark brown sugar and melted butter in a small bowl with a fork, then mix in the peanut butter and cinnamon until fairly smooth. Set aside.

3. Beat the granulated sugar and butter chunks in a large bowl with an electric mixer at medium speed until creamy and pale yellow, about 2 minutes. Beat in the eggs, one at a time, then scrape down the sides of the bowl and beat in the sour cream and vanilla. Turn off the beaters and add the flour mixture; beat at very low speed until smooth and light, about 1 minute.

4. Scoop out ¼ cup of the batter and stir it into the prepared peanut butter filling.

5. Pour about two-thirds of the remaining batter into the prepared Bundt pan, smoothing it evenly to the sides with a rubber spatula. Spoon the peanut butter mixture evenly over the batter and smooth it a bit with a rubber spatula. Take care not to press down too hard, and keep the peanut butter mixture in the center of the batter and away from the sides of the pan. Top with the remaining batter, again smoothing it to the sides of the pan to cover the filling completely.

6. Bake until golden brown, until a toothpick or cake tester inserted into the center of the cake comes out with a few moist crumbs attached (so long as it doesn't run into the filling inside), about 1 hour. Cool in the pan for 10 minutes, then up-end the cake onto a wire rack, remove the pan, and cool completely. The cake can be stored at room temperature, wrapped in plastic wrap or placed in a Bundt cake safe for up to 4 days. It can also be wrapped up tightly in plastic wrap and frozen for up to 2 months; unwrap the cake and allow it to stand on a wire rack until it comes to room temperature, about 45 minutes.

You can frost this Bundt cake with any number of frostings or icings. Try the Marshmallow Peanut Butter Frosting (page 175), the Peanut Butter Frosting (page 210), the Easy Peanut Butter Icing (page 197), Easy Vanilla Glaze (page 42), Easy Chocolate Frosting (page 164), or the Chocolate Glaze (page 189).

PEANUT BUTTER CARAMEL CORN

Why have ordinary caramel corn when you can coat the popcorn with a peanut butter caramel mixture? You'll need a candy thermometer to get the syrup to the right gooey, chewy consistency. Use fresh, air-popped popcorn for the best results.

MAKES ABOUT 1 POUND

Nonstick spray or unsalted butter for greasing the baking sheet

1 cup sugar

⅓ cup light corn syrup

¼ cup water

2 tablespoons unsulphured molasses (see page 13)

2 tablespoons creamy standard peanut butter

½ teaspoon baking soda

¼ teaspoon salt, optional

1 teaspoon vanilla extract

8 cups crushed popped popcorn (see Note)

1. Lightly spray or butter two large baking sheets and set them aside.

2. Mix the sugar, corn syrup, water, and molasses in a large, heavy-duty saucepan and set it over medium heat. Continue stirring until the sugar dissolves. Clip a candy thermometer to the side of the pan and cook the syrup, without stirring, until the thermometer registers 280°F (soft-crack stage—see page 25 for high-altitude candy-making tips).

3. Remove the pan from the heat and stir in the peanut butter, baking soda, and salt, if using. Be very careful: the mixture will roil up in the pan. Stir in the vanilla, then stir in the crushed popcorn. Pour the mixture out onto the prepared baking sheets, spreading it to the sides and breaking the kernels apart. Cool on a wire rack for at least 1 hour, then pour the caramel corn into resealable plastic bags and store, sealed tightly, at room temperature for up to 2 weeks.

NOTE: *For the best texture, the popcorn should be crushed—do it in batches between your hands so that it does not become powdery, but so the individual kernels are broken in three or four places.*

PEANUT BUTTER CHEESECAKE

Forget about those carb-phobes. You'll have people lining up for blocks to try this dense, decadent, and utterly wonderful cheesecake. It's best if you make it a day ahead and then let the flavors develop in the refrigerator overnight.

MAKES ONE 9-INCH CHEESECAKE (ABOUT 16 SERVINGS)

2 cups graham cracker crumbs

8 tablespoons (1 stick) unsalted butter, melted and cooled

2 tablespoons packed dark brown sugar

½ teaspoon ground cinnamon

¼ teaspoon salt

24 ounces cream cheese (regular or low-fat but not nonfat)

1⅓ cups granulated sugar

1 cup creamy standard peanut butter

4 large eggs, at room temperature

½ cup sour cream (regular or low-fat but not nonfat)

1 to 2 tablespoons vanilla extract

1. Position the rack in the center of the oven and preheat the oven to 350°F. Wrap the outside of a 9-inch springform pan tightly in aluminum foil (this will keep the water in the water bath from seeping into the batter as the cake bakes); set aside.

2. Stir the graham cracker crumbs, melted butter, brown sugar, cinnamon, and salt in a large bowl until the graham cracker crumbs are thoroughly moistened. Pour a little more than half of this mixture into the bottom of the prepared springform pan and press it all the way to the edges so that it coats the bottom of the pan. Pour the rest of the mixture around the inner seam of the pan, where the rim meets the bottom, and press the crust halfway up the sides of the pan, filling in along the bottom where necessary. Set aside.

3. Beat the cream cheese and granulated sugar in a large bowl with an electric mixer at medium speed until smooth, about 2 minutes. If you rub a small bit between your fingers, you should feel only a few sugar granules. Beat in the peanut butter. Scrape down the sides of the bowl with a rubber spatula, then beat in the eggs, one at a time, making sure each is thoroughly incorporated before adding the next. Finally, beat in the sour cream and vanilla.

4. Taking care not to disturb the crust, pour this mixture into the prepared pan. Smooth its top with a rubber spatula. Place the springform pan in a high-sided roasting pan that's large enough to accommodate it comfortably. Fill the pan with hot water until it comes about halfway up the outside of the springform pan.

5. Bake until the top is dry and lightly browned and the cake jiggles like a set custard when tapped, about 1½ hours. Cool in the pan for 10 minutes, then remove the springform pan from the water bath and cool it completely to room temperature on a wire rack.

6. Remove the foil and cover the pan with plastic wrap, taking care not to press the wrap onto the surface of the cheesecake. Refrigerate overnight.

7. Unlatch the sides and transfer to a serving platter. If desired, run a long knife between the bottom of the pan and the cake, then gently slide the cake onto the serving platter.

Customize It!

Add ⅔ cup semisweet or bittersweet chocolate chips with the vanilla.

Make an easy apricot or grape glaze by melting ½ cup of jam or jelly and 2 tablespoons water in a small saucepan set over low heat. Cool this mixture, then spoon and spread it gently over the cooled cheesecake once it's out of the pan, letting the glaze drip down the sides.

Make a fresh berry glaze by melting ¼ cup red currant jelly with 1 tablespoon water in a medium saucepan set over low heat; stir in 2 cups blueberries, raspberries, or sliced strawberries off the heat until the berries are coated and glistening.

Set aside to cool for 10 minutes, then spoon and spread this mixture on top of the cooled cheesecake once it's out of the pan.

Make a peanut butter banana cheesecake by substituting 2 teaspoons banana extract for the vanilla. Make a glaze for the top of the cake by melting ¼ cup white grape jelly and 1 tablespoon water in a medium saucepan set over low heat; stir in 2 ripe bananas, thinly sliced. Cool for 10 minutes, then spoon this mixture over the top of the cheesecake once it's out of the pan.

PEANUT BUTTER CREAM PUFFS WITH A CHOCOLATE GLAZE

These are traditional, airy cream puffs, light as a feather and filled with a rich peanut butter pastry cream.

MAKES 12 LARGE CREAM PUFFS

FOR THE CREAM PUFFS

1 cup water

½ stick (4 tablespoons) unsalted butter, plus additional for greasing the baking sheet

1 cup flour, plus additional for dusting the baking sheet

½ teaspoon salt

4 large eggs, at room temperature

FOR THE PEANUT BUTTER PASTRY CREAM

1½ cups plus 2 tablespoons milk, preferably low-fat or nonfat

4 large egg yolks, at room temperature

½ cup sugar

5 tablespoons all-purpose flour

½ cup creamy standard peanut butter

2 teaspoons vanilla extract

FOR THE CHOCOLATE GLAZE

4 ounces semisweet chocolate, chopped

½ stick (4 tablespoons) unsalted butter, cut into chunks

1 tablespoon white or gold rum

1. To make the cream puffs, heat the water in a medium saucepan over medium heat just until it's lukewarm, about 98°F. Add the butter and melt it in the water. Stir in the flour and salt until thick, then reduce the heat to low and continue cooking, stirring all the while, until the mixture is soft but pulls together into a ball and leaves a film around the edges of the pan, 5 to 6 minutes. The dough should not feel sticky to your fingers. Transfer this dough to a large bowl; cool for 10 minutes.

2. Use an electric mixer at medium speed to beat the eggs into the dough one at a time, adding another egg only after the one before it has been thoroughly incorporated into the dough. You should end up with a smooth, shiny dough.

3. Butter and flour a large baking sheet or line it with a silicone baking mat. Gather up about 2 tablespoons of the dough and place it on the baking sheet, shaping it something like a Ping-Pong ball. Continue making the balls until you have used all the dough. Set the baking tray aside at room temperature for 20 minutes to dry the balls somewhat. Meanwhile, position the rack in the center of the oven and preheat the oven to 375°F.

4. Bake until puffed and golden, about 35 minutes. Turn off the oven, open the door, and leave them in the oven on the baking tray for about 1 hour to dry out a bit. After that, remove the tray to a wire rack and cool the puffs completely to room temperature, about 1 more hour.

5. Meanwhile, make the peanut butter pastry cream. Heat ½ cup of the milk in a medium saucepan set over medium heat until small bubbles fizz along the pan's inner rim. While the milk's heating, whisk the egg yolks and sugar in a medium bowl until thick and pale yellow, about 2 minutes. Whisk in the flour until smooth, then whisk in the peanut butter.

6. Once the milk is hot enough, whisk about half of it into the egg yolk and peanut butter mixture. Then whisk this combined mixture back into the pan with the remaining hot milk. Turn the heat down to very low (if you're using an electric stove, use a second burner just now set to low) and continue cooking and whisking until the mixture has thickened somewhat and can coat the back of a wooden spoon, about 2 minutes. Strain this mixture through a fine-mesh sieve into a clean medium bowl (so you can remove any bits of egg yolk that have inadvertently scrambled over the heat), then whisk in the remaining 1 cup plus 2 tablespoons milk and the vanilla. Set aside to cool at room temperature, about 20 minutes. (You can make the peanut butter pastry cream in advance; once it's cooled, store it tightly covered in the refrigerator for up to 2 days in advance.)

7. Once the cream puffs and the pastry cream have cooled, cut the top third off each puff and set these tops aside. Scoop out any extraneous dough from the shells, then fill each with 2 to 3 tablespoons peanut butter pastry cream. Place the tops back on the cream puffs and return them to the wire rack.

8. Make an easy glaze for the cream puffs by melting the chocolate and butter in the top half of a double boiler set over medium heat, stirring constantly; or in a bowl in the microwave, heating it on high and stirring the mixture every 15 seconds. In either case, melt the chocolate and butter until half the chocolate has melted, then remove the top half of the double boiler from over the heat or the bowl from the microwave and continue stirring away from the heat until all the chocolate has melted. Set aside to cool for 5 minutes, then stir in the rum.

9. Lay wax paper across your work surface, then set the filled cream puffs on their wire rack over the wax paper. Drizzle a scant tablespoon of the chocolate glaze over each cream puff (any glaze that drips off the puffs will be caught by the wax paper). Set the puffs aside to let the glaze harden, about 15 minutes. Serve at once, or store them in a tightly sealed container at room temperature for no more than 1 day.

Customize It!

Flavor the pastry cream by adding 1 teaspoon maple or rum extract with the vanilla; or substitute 2 teaspoons banana extract or 1 teaspoon orange extract for the vanilla. Omit the Chocolate Glaze and top the cream puffs with the Easy Vanilla Glaze (page 42) or Orange Glaze (page 31).

PEANUT BUTTER CRÈME BRULÉE

Acrunchy top you have to crack open with a spoon to get to a rich peanut butter custard underneath—we ask you, is there anything better?

MAKES 4 SERVINGS

5 large egg yolks, at room temperature

⅓ cup plus ¼ cup sugar

1 cup milk, preferably low-fat

½ cup creamy standard peanut butter

1. Position the rack in the center of the oven; preheat the oven to 350°F. Bring a large saucepan of water or a teapot of water to a low simmer over high heat.

2. Whisk the egg yolks and ⅓ cup of the sugar in a large bowl until creamy and pale yellow, about 2 minutes. Whisk in the milk and peanut butter until smooth and silky. Divide this mixture into 4 heat-safe custard cups or broiler-proof ramekins. Place these in a large baking pan, such as a 9 × 13-inch pan. Pour the simmering water into the baking dish, taking care not to get any water in the custards, until the water comes about halfway up the cups or ramekins.

3. Bake the custards in this water bath until lightly browned and set, about 35 minutes. Remove the pan with the custards from the oven, then carefully remove the custard cups from the pan and place them on a wire rack to cool completely. (The dish can be made up to this point up to 2 days in advance; once the custards are cool, cover them with plastic wrap and store in the refrigerator.)

4. Sprinkle 1 tablespoon of the remaining sugar evenly over each custard. Preheat the broiler and place the broiler pan about 5 inches from the heat source. Place the custards on a baking sheet and broil them until the sugar caramelizes and begins to bubble, about 3 minutes. Alternatively, you can use a kitchen blowtorch to caramelize the sugar on each custard—just make sure you get all the granules, even the ones at the sides. Place the custards in the refrigerator and chill at least 1 hour, until the custard itself is cold and the sugar coating has hardened completely. Serve each with a spoon; crack the crust open as you enjoy the pudding underneath.

PEANUT BUTTER CRUNCH SHEET CAKE

Look no further for the next hit at your next family gathering, potluck, or office party: the ultimate sheet cake, a light, moist cake that's made in a jelly-roll pan and then given a chocolate chip crunch topping.

MAKES ONE 10 × 17-INCH CAKE (ABOUT 24 SERVINGS)

3¼ cups all-purpose flour, plus additional for dusting the pan

1 tablespoon baking powder

1½ teaspoons baking soda

½ teaspoon salt, optional

16 tablespoons (2 sticks) cool unsalted butter, cut into chunks, plus additional for greasing the pan

1 cup packed dark brown sugar

½ cup creamy standard peanut butter

½ cup corn syrup

4 large eggs, at room temperature

1 tablespoon vanilla extract

1½ cups buttermilk (regular or low-fat, but not nonfat)

1½ cups granulated sugar

1 cup crunchy standard peanut butter

2 cups semisweet chocolate chips

1. Position the rack in the center of the oven and preheat the oven to 375°F. Lightly butter and flour a 10 × 17-inch jelly-roll pan; set aside. Whisk 3 cups flour, the baking powder, baking soda, and salt, if using, in a large bowl until the baking powder and baking soda are evenly distributed in the flour; set aside.

2. Beat the butter, brown sugar, creamy peanut butter, and corn syrup in a second large bowl with an electric mixer at medium speed until creamy and smooth, about 3 minutes, scraping down the sides of the bowl a few times to make sure everything's evenly mixed. Admittedly, this job is tough for a hand-held mixer; if you have one, occasionally turn the beaters off and use them to cut the various ingredients into each other before you continue beating.

3. Beat in the eggs, one at a time, making sure each is thoroughly incorporated before adding the next. Beat in the vanilla until smooth.

4. Beat in ½ cup of the buttermilk, then turn off the beaters and add a third of the prepared flour mixture. Beat at a very low speed until combined, then beat in another ½ cup buttermilk. Again, turn off the beaters, add about half the remaining flour mixture, and beat at a very low speed until combined. Finally, beat in the remaining buttermilk, then turn off the beaters, remove them from the batter, and stir the remaining flour mixture in with a wooden spoon or a rubber spatula, just until combined (there may be some graininess from the flour in the batter but there should be no white flour visible). Spoon and spread this mixture into the prepared jelly-roll pan, using a rubber spatula or an offset icing spatula to move it gently in all the corners and against the sides.

5. In a medium bowl, mix the granulated sugar, crunchy peanut butter, chocolate chips, and the remaining ¼ cup flour until the consistency of a crumbly muffin topping. A fork is the best tool for this job, although you can use a whisk. Crumble this mixture evenly over the top of the batter in the pan.

6. Bake until golden and a toothpick inserted into the cake (but missing the melted chocolate chips) comes out with a few moist crumbs attached, about 30 minutes. Cool the cake in the pan on a rack for at least 20 minutes before cutting it. Once completely cooled, the cake may be wrapped in the pan with plastic wrap and stored at room temperature for up to 3 days.

Customize It!

Add ⅔ cup chopped dried apples, dried blueberries, dried cranberries, or dried raisins, or ½ cup cocoa nibs into the cake batter with the last addition of the flour.

Substitute white chocolate chips for the semisweet ones.

Add ¾ cup chopped pecans, chopped unsalted roasted peanuts, or chopped walnuts to the topping with the chocolate chips.

PEANUT BUTTER CUPCAKES WITH A EASY PEANUT BUTTER ICING

Loaded with peanut butter, these cupcakes are nevertheless so light, you'll swear they're going to levitate off the plate. The icing only has three ingredients and it's very spreadable—great for many other cakes, muffins, or quick-bread loaves in this book.

MAKES 18 CUPCAKES

FOR THE PEANUT BUTTER CUPCAKES

18 paper muffin cups

2 cups all-purpose flour

2 teaspoons baking powder

½ teaspoon salt

½ cup creamy standard peanut butter

6 tablespoons cool unsalted butter, cut into chunks

1 cup packed light brown sugar

⅓ cup granulated sugar

1 large egg plus 2 large egg yolks, at room temperature

1 teaspoon vanilla extract

1 cup milk, preferably low-fat or nonfat

FOR THE EASY PEANUT BUTTER ICING

3 tablespoons crunchy standard peanut butter

3 tablespoons milk, preferably low-fat or nonfat

1 cup confectioners' sugar, or a little more depending on the day's humidity

1. Position the rack in the center of the oven and preheat it to 350°F. Line 18 indentations in the muffin tin with the paper muffin cups; set aside. (If you don't have an 18-cup muffin tin, use two standard 12-cup tins, filling only half of the second tin's indentations with batter. Fill the other indentations halfway with hot water just before baking.) Whisk the flour, baking powder, and salt in a medium bowl until the baking powder and salt are evenly distributed in the flour; set aside.

2. Beat the creamy peanut butter and butter in a large bowl using an electric mixer at medium speed until light, about 2 minutes, scraping down the sides of the bowl as necessary with a rubber spatula. Beat in the brown sugar and granulated sugar until the mixture is pale brown and smooth, about 2 more minutes. Beat in the egg, egg yolks, and vanilla until silky.

3. Using the mixer at very low speed, beat in half the milk until smooth, then half the prepared flour mixture. Scrape down the sides of the bowl and beat in the remaining milk, then the remaining flour mixture, just until incorporated. Do not beat more than 30 seconds after you add the last bit of flour or the cupcakes will be tough. Divide the batter evenly among the muffin cups, filling them each about three-quarters full.

4. Bake until lightly brown and firm to the touch, about 25 minutes. A toothpick inserted into one of the cupcakes should come out with a few moist crumbs attached. Cool the cupcakes in the pans on a wire rack for 5 minutes, then remove them from the pans and continue cooling the cupcakes on the wire rack for 1 hour. They can be stored this way, unfrosted, at room temperature in a sealed bag or plastic container for up to 3 days; or they can be frozen for up to 3 months in a sealed bag or container—simply defrost them for 15 minutes on a wire rack before icing.

5. To make the Easy Peanut Butter Icing, whisk the peanut butter and milk in a large bowl until smooth. Whisk in the confectioners' sugar in ¼-cup increments until a smooth icing forms; you may have to add a few more tablespoons of confectioners' sugar on a dry day. Spread about 1½ teaspoons of the icing on each cooled cupcake just before you serve them.

Customize It!

Add 1 teaspoon banana, maple, or rum extract with the vanilla.

Stir ⅔ cup semisweet chocolate chips or ½ cup chopped nuts or chopped roasted unsalted peanuts into the batter with the second addition of the flour mixture.

PEANUT BUTTER CUPS

Here's the classic candy, a chocolaty cup filled with a toothy peanut butter filling. You'll need a pastry brush to paint the melted chocolate into the cups.

MAKES 24 CANDIES

24 ounces milk chocolate, roughly chopped, or 24 ounces milk chocolate chips

24 small candy cups, preferably foil candy cups (see suppliers in the Source Guide, pages 237–38)

¾ cup creamy standard peanut butter

½ cup confectioners' sugar

2 tablespoons powdered nonfat dry milk

2 teaspoons vanilla extract

1. Place three-quarters of the chocolate in the top half of a double boiler set over about 2 inches of simmering water. If you don't have a double boiler, put the chocolate in a large bowl that will fit securely over a large saucepan with about the same amount of simmering water. Adjust the heat so the water simmers slowly, then stir the chocolate until about half of it has melted. Remove the top half of the double boiler or the bowl from the heat—watch out for escaping steam that can burn your fingers—and add the remainder of the chopped chocolate. Continue stirring away from the heat until all the chocolate has melted. Set aside to cool until a small drop of chocolate, dripped onto your work surface, holds its shape and doesn't run, about 5 minutes.

2. Use a small pastry brush to paint this melted milk chocolate into the foil or paper candy cups. Be generous without being sloppy—make about a ¼-inch layer of chocolate all around the inside of the cups. As you finish them, place them on a large baking sheet. Once you're all done, place the baking sheet and all the cups in the refrigerator to chill for 10 minutes, just so the chocolate hardens. Place the remaining chocolate in the double boiler or the bowl over the saucepan with the hot water, now removed from the burner (the hot water will keep the chocolate from setting up).

3. Meanwhile, mash the peanut butter into the confectioners' sugar, powdered nonfat dry milk, and vanilla in a medium bowl until a grainy, somewhat dry, almost sandy paste forms. It's not sticky, but it is stiff.

4. Once the chocolate has hardened in the cups, scoop up about 2 teaspoons of the peanut butter filling and place it in one cup, gently pressing it into place so that it forms an even filling in the cup with a fairly even top surface. Continue filling all the cups.

5. Transfer the remaining melted milk chocolate to a measuring cup with a handle and spout. Pour the chocolate over the peanut butter centers, filling the cups to the top and sealing in the filling. Alternatively, you can spoon the melted chocolate onto the cups to create even, smooth tops on them.

6. Let the cups rest at room temperature until the chocolate has set, about 3 hours. You can speed up this process by placing the cups on their baking sheet in the refrigerator for 5 minutes, then returning it to room temperature. Store the cups in an airtight container between sheets of wax paper for up to 2 weeks.

Customize Them!

Substitute bittersweet, semisweet, or white chocolate for the milk chocolate.

Substitute 2 teaspoons grated orange zest for the vanilla in the filling.

Make a half recipe of the peanut butter filling. Place only 1 teaspoon of it in each cup, then top with 1 teaspoon grape, raspberry, or strawberry jelly, or 1 teaspoon Marshmallow Fluff or Marshmallow Crème. Be very gentle as you pour the melted chocolate onto the tops to seal these cups.

PEANUT BUTTER DESSERT BURRITO

few years ago, the California Milk Advisory Board asked us to put together various ice cream sundaes that represent the large cities in the state. For San Diego, we came up with the concept of an ice cream burrito—and it turned into a summer hit that year. Here it is, reinterpreted with (what else?) peanut butter.

MAKES 4 DESSERT BURRITOS

4 ounces bittersweet or semisweet chocolate, chopped

¼ creamy standard peanut butter

Four 10-inch flour tortillas

¼ teaspoon ground cinnamon

1 quart vanilla ice cream

1. Place the chocolate in the top half of a double boiler set over about an inch of simmering water in the bottom half or in a medium bowl that fits snugly over a medium saucepan set over medium heat with about an inch of slowly simmering water. Adjust the heat so the water simmers slowly, then stir the chocolate with a heat-safe rubber spatula or a wooden spoon until half of it has melted. Remove the double boiler's top half from the heat—be careful of escaping steam that can burn your fingers—and continue stirring until all the chocolate has melted and the mixture is smooth. Alternatively, you can melt the chocolate in a small bowl in the microwave—place it in the bowl, then heat it in 15-second increments on high until half of it has melted; after that, continue stirring it out of the microwave until all the chocolate has melted. In either case, cool the melted chocolate for 5 minutes.

2. Add the peanut butter to the chocolate and whisk until smooth.

3. Warm the tortillas by placing them between two plates (the top one inverted so that the concave surfaces of the plates face each other) and heating them in the microwave on high for 10 to 15 seconds.

4. Assemble the burritos by laying the tortillas on each of four plates. Spread about a quarter of the chocolate mixture on each tortilla (about 2 tablespoons on each). Sprinkle a pinch of cinnamon over each tortilla. Place two ½-cup scoops of ice cream in the center of each tortilla. Fold the burritos closed by folding them in half shut, closing the pointy ends slightly, then rolling the burritos closed. Serve at once.

Customize Them!

You can substitute any flavor of ice cream you prefer: vanilla swirl, banana, peanut butter, chocolate, strawberry—your imagination's the limit.

PEANUT BUTTER FUDGE, THE CLASSIC VERSION

The real money must be in fudge. There's a store selling the stuff in every tourist town across America. Or perhaps it's just that everyone loves fudge, that chocolaty confection that used to be synonymous with the holidays and has now morphed into a vacation treat.

MAKES 16 PIECES OF FUDGE

1⅔ cups whole milk

4 ounces unsweetened chocolate, roughly chopped

4 cups sugar

2 tablespoons light corn syrup

¼ teaspoon salt, optional

⅔ cup creamy standard peanut butter

1 tablespoon vanilla extract

1. Place the milk and chocolate in a large saucepan set over very low heat. Stirring constantly, melt the chocolate in the milk, removing the pan from the heat every once in a while to keep the chocolate from scorching; continue stirring even when the pan is off the heat.

2. Stir in the sugar, corn syrup, and salt, if using. Continue cooking, stirring all the while, until the sugar has dissolved. Clip a candy thermometer to the inside of the pan without its touching the bottom and raise the heat to medium. Continue cooking, stirring frequently, until the temperature reaches 234°F (or "soft-ball stage," as sometimes marked on the thermometer—see Note on page 25 for high-altitude tips).

3. Remove the pan from the heat at once and set it aside until the bottom of the pan is lukewarm to the touch and the thermometer registers 110°F, about 1 hour or a little more, depending on how warm your kitchen is.

4. The moment it reaches 110°F, use an electric mixer to beat in the peanut butter and vanilla. Continue beating just until the fudge loses its glossy finish and looks a little dull. Do not overbeat—it will solidify, crystallize, and become grainy. It begins to crystallize the moment it loses its sheen, so that's the moment you want to quit beating.

5. Line a 9-inch pan with wax paper or plastic wrap and spread the fudge in the pan, smoothing it gently to the corners with a rubber spatula. Set the pan on a wire rack to cool for 20 minutes, then place it in the refrigerator and continue cooling at least 3 hours or overnight. Once the pan is completely cool, you can cover it with plastic wrap to keep the fudge from drying out.

6. Turn the pan upside down onto a cutting board and use the wax paper or plastic wrap to wiggle the fudge out of the pan. Remove the pan, peel off the wax paper or plastic wrap, and cut the fudge into sixteen pieces, making three equidistant cuts in each of two parallel directions in the block. Wrap these individual pieces in small pieces of wax paper or in candy wrappers, available at baking supply stores or from candy supply stores on the web or listed in the Source Guide (pages 237–38). Wrapped and placed in an airtight container, the pieces will stay fresh for up to 1 week.

Customize It!

Reduce the vanilla to 2 teaspoons and add 1 teaspoon banana, rum, or maple extract. Just before you're done beating the fudge and ready to smooth it into the pan, beat in ½ cup chopped pecans, chopped honey-roasted peanuts, chopped roasted unsalted peanuts, or chopped walnuts.

PEANUT BUTTER FUDGE, QUICK VERSION

Henk's European Deli and Bakery is an excellent Dutch deli in Dallas, Texas, right down Blackwell Street from Northpark Mall. At the candy counter, master confectioner Jamie Collins makes some of the best peanut butter fudge around, and she's been generous enough to supply her quick and easy recipe for this book.

MAKES 16 PIECES OF FUDGE

Unsalted butter for greasing the pan
1 pound confectioners' sugar
½ cup evaporated milk
One (7-ounce) jar Marshmallow Fluff or Marshmallow Crème (see page 10)
1 cup creamy standard peanut butter

1. Use a small pat of butter on a piece of wax paper to grease an 8-inch-square pan; set aside.

2. Place the confectioners' sugar and milk in a large saucepan, put it over medium-low heat, and stir until the sugar dissolves. Raise the heat to medium, clip a candy thermometer to the inside of the pan, and continue cooking, stirring occasionally, until the temperature reaches 234°F, about 4 to 5 minutes. (That temperature is often marked "soft-ball stage" on a candy thermometer—see page 25 for tips on high-altitude candy making.)

3. Remove the pan from the heat and quickly stir in the Marshmallow Fluff or Marshmallow Crème and peanut butter. Use an electric mixer at medium speed to beat the mixture until smooth. Pour into the prepared pan and smooth to the edges. Set the pan aside at room temperature until the fudge sets, 2 to 3 hours.

4. Turn the pan upside down onto a cutting board and rap it a few times to release the fudge. Remove the pan and cut the fudge into sixteen pieces. Wrap each one in a small piece of wax paper or a candy wrapper. Store the wrapped pieces in an airtight container for up to 4 days at room temperature.

Customize It!

Stir in ½ cup chopped pecans, chopped roasted unsalted peanuts, chopped skinned hazelnuts, chopped walnuts, or cocoa nibs just before you pour the mixture into the pan. Flavor the fudge with 2 teaspoons banana, maple, rum, or vanilla extract, or 1 teaspoon orange extract.

PEANUT BUTTER ICE CREAM

In our first book in this series, *The Ultimate Ice Cream Book*, there's a recipe for peanut butter ice cream, but the emphasis there is on the silky cream, not necessarily the peanut butter. Here, we've put as much peanut butter into the ice cream custard as it can possibly hold. The result? One fabulous treat on a hot summer afternoon.

MAKES 1 QUART (CAN BE DOUBLED FOR HALF-GALLON ICE CREAM MAKERS)

½ cup packed light brown sugar

¼ cup granulated sugar

2 large eggs plus 2 large egg yolks, at room temperature

1½ cups whole milk

½ cup creamy standard peanut butter

1 cup heavy cream

1 tablespoon vanilla extract

¼ teaspoon salt, optional

1. Beat the brown sugar, granulated sugar, eggs, and egg yolks in a large bowl with an electric mixer at medium speed until thick and pale yellow, about 3 minutes. Set aside.

2. Heat the milk in a medium saucepan set over medium heat, just until small bubbles pop up around the pan's inner edge. Using the mixer at medium speed, beat about half the hot milk into the egg mixture, then beat this combined mixture back into the remaining milk in the saucepan. Reduce the heat to low and cook, stirring constantly, just until the mixture can coat the back of the spoon, about 2 minutes—that is, dip the wooden spoon in the custard, then run your finger through the custard on the spoon's back; the custard should be thick enough that the line you create will stay dry and its borders intact even when you turn the spoon upside down or tilt it on an angle. If you want to be extra-cautious about egg safety, you can clip a candy thermometer to the side of the pan and cook the egg custard until it reaches 165°F, stirring constantly.

3. Remove the pan from the heat and whisk in the peanut butter. Strain the ice cream custard through a fine-mesh sieve into a large bowl to get rid of any bits of inadvertently scrambled egg. Stir in the heavy cream, vanilla, and salt, if using. Place the mixture in your refrigerator to chill for at least 4 hours or overnight.

4. Freeze the ice cream in an ice-cream machine according to the manufacturer's instructions. Serve at once.

Customize It!

Peanut Butter and Jelly Ice Cream Soften ¼ cup grape, raspberry, or strawberry jelly in a small saucepan set over low heat, stirring constantly. Cool for 10 minutes. Spoon or dispense the finished ice cream into a container while drizzling in the softened jelly, thereby creating ribbons of it in the ice cream.

Peanut Butter Chip Ice Cream Add ⅔ cup chocolate chips or 4 ounces semisweet or bittersweet chocolate, shaved, into the machine during the final few turns of the peanut butter ice cream.

Peanut Butter Fudge Swirl Ice Cream Spoon or dispense the finished ice cream into a container while also spooning in purchased chocolate sauce, thereby creating a swirl pattern in the ice cream.

Thanksgiving Peanut Butter Ice Cream Add 1 teaspoon ground cinnamon, ¼ teaspoon grated nutmeg, and ¼ teaspoon ground allspice with the vanilla. Stir ½ cup mini marshmallows into the ice cream during the last few turns in the machine, just as it's finishing up.

PEANUT BUTTER LAYER CAKE WITH A PEANUT BUTTER FROSTING

Recently, layer cakes have become the fad in New York City. Bakeries are popping up all over town, each specializing in rich cakes with buttercream frosting. Here's our peanut butter homage to this suddenly hip American cake—complete with a simplified buttercream-style frosting.

MAKES ONE 3-TIER LAYER CAKE (ABOUT 12 SERVINGS)

FOR THE PEANUT BUTTER LAYER CAKE

2½ cups all-purpose flour, plus additional for dusting the pans

1½ tablespoons baking powder

½ teaspoon salt, optional

¾ cup packed light brown sugar

¾ cup granulated sugar

8 tablespoons (1 stick) cool unsalted butter, cut into chunks, plus additional
  for greasing the pans

½ cup creamy standard peanut butter

4 large eggs, at room temperature

1 tablespoon vanilla extract

1 cup milk (regular, low-fat, or nonfat)

FOR THE PEANUT BUTTER FROSTING

1½ cups creamy standard peanut butter

8 tablespoons (1 stick) unsalted butter, softened

¼ cup solid vegetable shortening

3 cups confectioners' sugar

1 tablespoon vanilla extract

2 to 3 tablespoons milk (regular, low-fat, or nonfat)

1. After positioning the rack in the center of the oven, preheat the oven to 350°F. Lightly butter and flour three 9-inch-round cake pans; set aside. Whisk the flour, baking powder, and salt, if using, in a medium bowl to get the baking powder and salt evenly distributed in the flour; set aside.

2. Beat the brown sugar, granulated sugar, butter, and peanut butter in a large bowl, using an electric mixer at medium speed, until smooth and light, about 3 minutes. Scrape down the sides of the bowl occasionally as the mixture beats to ensure the sugar's evenly distributed in the mixture. Beat in the eggs, one at a time, then the vanilla.

3. Beat in ½ cup of the milk. Turn off the beaters, add half the prepared flour mixture, then beat it in at a very low speed, just until incorporated. Add the remaining ½ cup milk, continue beating at low speed, then add the remainder of the flour mixture, and beat just until a smooth batter forms without much graininess from the flour. Do not overbeat—simply get all the visible white from the flour incorporated without turning the batter sticky or stringy. Divide the dough evenly among the three prepared cake pans and gently spread it to the edges with a rubber spatula.

4. Bake until lightly browned and a toothpick inserted into the center of one of the cakes comes out with a few moist crumbs attached, about 30 minutes. Cool the pans on a wire rack for 10 minutes, then unmold them by placing a rack or a large cutting board over them one at a time, inverting the pan and the rack or board, tapping the cake loose, removing the pan, and then placing another rack over the cake layer so you can reinvert it top side up. Cool all the layers out of the pan on the rack until they are room temperature, about 1 hour, maybe a little longer.

5. To make the Peanut Butter Frosting, beat the peanut butter, butter, and shortening in a large bowl with an electric mixer at medium speed (using clean beaters, of course) until smooth and creamy, about 2 minutes. Beat in the confectioners' sugar in ½-cup increments, then beat in the vanilla. Beat in just enough milk to make a smooth, spreadable frosting—not too much or the frosting will be runny.

6. Use a long, thin knife to slice the slightly rounded tops off the three cake layers; discard these tops or save them for the kids to munch on. Place one of the cake layers cut side up on a cake plate or decorative stand. Cut long, thin strips of wax paper and slip them under the cake layer—these will protect the cake plate from frosting smudges as you ice it. Spread about ¼ of the frosting over the top layer with an offset icing spatula or a long thin knife, then top with a second cake layer, cut side up. Spread about ⅓ of the remaining frosting over this next layer, then top with the last cake layer, again top side up. Spread about ½ of the remaining frosting over the top of the cake. Use the remainder of the frosting to ice the sides of the cake—take care that you don't drag pieces of the cake into the frosting; it may help to dip the spatula or knife in water at this point to make the frosting more spreadable. Once the cake is frosted, remove the strips of wax paper. Serve at once, or place in a cake-safe container or put a deep large-lidded container over the cake—or stick toothpicks in the cake and lightly drape plastic wrap over the whole cake to keep it moist; it should stay covered like this at room temperature for up to 2 days.

Customize It!

Add 1 teaspoon banana extract to the cake batter with the vanilla. Slice 2 medium bananas and arrange these decoratively over the top of the cake just before you serve it.

Slice 1 pint of ripe strawberries and lay these decoratively over the top of the cake before you serve it.

Sprinkle the top of the cake with ½ cup semisweet chocolate chips or ¼ cup cocoa nibs.

Shave 2 ounces of semisweet or bittersweet chocolate with a cheese plane or through the holes of a box grater; sprinkle some of these shavings on the frosting between each layer of cake, then sprinkle the rest of the shavings over the top and sides of the cake.

Sprinkle 1 cup sweetened shredded coconut over the top and sides of the frosted cake.

PEANUT BUTTER MERINGUE PIE

Here's a peanut butter take on a great American pie: a creamy, pudding-like filling under an airy meringue. For an easier recipe, simply use a store-bought pie shell, baked as directed on the package's instructions.

MAKES ONE 9-INCH PIE (ABOUT 8 SERVINGS)

FOR THE CRUST

1 cup all-purpose flour, plus additional for dusting

¼ teaspoon salt

⅓ cup plus 1 tablespoon solid vegetable shortening

¼ teaspoon apple cider vinegar

3 to 5 tablespoons cold water

FOR THE FILLING AND MERINGUE

4 large eggs, separated, at room temperature

¾ cup creamy standard peanut butter

2 teaspoons vanilla extract

2½ cups milk, preferably low-fat or nonfat

½ cup plus ⅓ cup sugar

¼ cup powdered nonfat dry milk

3 tablespoons cornstarch

½ teaspoon cream of tartar

¼ teaspoon salt

1. Position the rack in the center of the oven and preheat the oven to 400°F.

2. To make the piecrust, mix the flour and salt in a medium bowl. Cut in the shortening with a pastry cutter or a fork until the mixture resembles very coarse meal. Sprinkle on the vinegar, then add the water in 1-tablespoon increments, stirring each in with a fork until a dough begins to form. Do not make this dough too wet—you just want it to cohere.

3. Place a few drops of water on your work surface, then line it with wax paper (the water will keep the paper in place). Dust the paper lightly with flour, then turn the dough onto the wax paper. Gather the dough into a ball, then dust both it and your rolling pin with flour. Roll the pastry crust to a circle about 10 inches in diameter. If you hold a 9-inch pie plate over it, you can tell if it's big enough to cover the bottom and come up the sides. Gently peel the wax paper and the dough together off your work surface, then invert them into the pie plate, centering the crust in the plate. Peel off the wax paper, then push the dough down to fill the plate. Cut off the ragged edges so the crust is even with the top of the plate; if desired, crimp the edge into a decorative pattern, or press down into the top edge with a fork to create a pattern. Line the piecrust with nonstick aluminum foil, then fill it with pie weights or dried beans. Bake until golden and firm, 6 to 8 minutes. Cool on a wire rack for 10 minutes, then pull off the foil and weights and continue cooling for 20 minutes. (If you used beans, they are no longer good for cooking but can be used again and again to bake pie and tart crusts in this manner.) Maintain the oven's temperature.

4. To make the filling, whisk the egg yolks, peanut butter, and vanilla in a medium bowl until fairly smooth; set aside.

5. Clean and dry the whisk, then whisk the milk, ⅓ cup sugar, and the powdered nonfat milk in a medium saucepan set over medium heat. Whisk in the cornstarch and continue cooking, whisking all the while, until the mixture comes to a very low simmer and thickens considerably.

6. Whisk about a third of this milk mixture into the egg yolk mixture, then whisk that combined mixture back into the milk mixture remaining in the saucepan. Cook over very low heat, whisking all the while, for 1 minute, or just until the first bubbles of a simmer appear. Pour into the prepared pie shell and set aside on a wire rack to cool.

7. Meanwhile, beat the egg whites, cream of tartar, and salt in a large bowl with an electric mixer at high speed, until foamy. Continue beating at high speed until soft peaks form. Beat in the remaining ½ cup sugar in four additions, scraping down the bowl after each. Continue beating at high speed until glossy, droopy, smooth peaks form right in the place where you lift the turned-off beaters out of the mixture. Use a rubber spatula to mound this meringue topping over the pie filling, sealing it all the way around against the piecrust by pressing down with the spatula or using your cleaned fingers. Make sure the meringue has no gaping holes in the top, but work gently so as not to push down and cause it to lose its poof.

8. Bake until the meringue is lightly browned, 5 to 7 minutes. Cool the pie on a wire rack at least 20 minutes before serving. Once completely cooled, the pie may be wrapped loosely with plastic wrap and stored in the refrigerator for up to 2 days.

Customize It!

Thinly slice 1 ripe banana, then lay these slices in the baked pie shell before pouring in the peanut butter filling.

Make half a recipe of the Easy Grape Jelly Sauce (page 225); spoon this into the baked pie shell before pouring in the peanut butter filling.

Melt 2 ounces of chopped semisweet or bittersweet in a small bowl in the microwave on high, stirring it after every 15-second increment until half the chocolate has melted. Remove the bowl and continue stirring until all the chocolate has melted. Cool for 5 minutes, then paint this melted chocolate into the baked pie shell. Set aside for 10 minutes to harden somewhat before pouring in the prepared pie filling.

PEANUT BUTTER MOUSSE

Most recipes for peanut butter mousse involve a beaten mixture of cream cheese and confectioners' sugar—an easy take, no doubt—but why not treat yourself to the real thing once in a while? Since this creamy mousse is prepared the traditional way (that is, with raw egg whites), use only organic eggs, or better still, use pasteurized eggs in their shells.

MAKES 8 SERVINGS

One ¼-ounce envelope unflavored gelatin

¼ cup cool water

4 large eggs, separated, at room temperature

1 cup heavy cream

⅔ cup sugar

¼ cup white or gold rum

1 cup creamy standard peanut butter

1 tablespoon vanilla extract

1. Sprinkle the gelatin over the water in a small bowl or teacup; set aside to soften for 5 minutes.

2. Meanwhile, beat the egg whites in a large bowl with an electric mixer at high speed until soft, droopy peaks form; set aside.

3. Clean and dry the beaters. Beat the cream in a cold medium bowl until it's whipped, light, and soft, with delicate peaks, about 2 minutes. Set aside. Clean and dry the beaters again.

4. Place the egg yolks and sugar in a bowl that will fit securely over a saucepan that has about 2 inches of simmering water in it. Reduce the heat so the water simmers slowly and begin beating the mixture with an electric mixer at medium speed until the sugar dissolves, about 1 minute (be careful of the electric cord around the heating element and the simmering water). Add the rum and continue beating over the simmering water until very thick, so thick in fact that the mixture, when dribbled off the stopped beaters, makes ribbons that do not immediately dissolve back into the mixture, about 4 more minutes. Remove the bowl from the heat—be careful of escaping steam—and beat in the peanut butter and vanilla until smooth.

5. Use a rubber spatula to fold the whipped cream gently into the peanut butter mixture. Then fold in the beaten egg very gently, using long, flowing arcs to make sure the egg whites do not deflate as they are incorporated into the mousse.

6. Pour the mousse into 8 wineglasses or a 1½- or 2-quart high-sided soufflé dish. Refrigerate until cold, for at least 4 hours; then cover the glasses or the soufflé dish with plastic wrap and store in the refrigerator until you're ready to serve the mousse, up to 2 days after you make it.

Customize It!

Substitute an almond-flavored liqueur such as Amaretto, butterscotch schnapps, coconut rum, a coffee-flavored liqueur such as Kahlúa, or whisky for the white or gold rum. Reduce the sugar to ⅓ cup and add ⅓ cup honey or maple syrup with the remaining sugar.

PEANUT BUTTER PARFAIT

Here's the ultimate peanut butter sundae, an over-the-top concoction of ice cream, caramel sauce, chocolate sauce, peanut butter, and salted peanuts. Have long-handled iced-tea spoons at the ready to get every drop out of those tall parfait glasses.

MAKES 4 PARFAITS

⅔ cup crunchy standard peanut butter

½ cup purchased chocolate syrup (do not use hot fudge topping)

¼ cup heavy cream

1 pint vanilla ice cream, softened for 5 minutes at room temperature

½ cup purchased caramel sauce

2 tablespoons chopped salted roasted peanuts

1. Mix the peanut butter and chocolate syrup in a small bowl with a fork until smooth; set aside. Whip the cream in a cold, medium bowl using an electric mixer at high speed until soft peaks form; set aside.

2. Place a small scoop (about 1 ounce or 2 tablespoons) of vanilla ice cream in the bottom of 4 parfait glasses. Top each of these scoops with 1 tablespoon caramel sauce and 1 tablespoon of the chocolate/peanut butter sauce. Place a slightly larger scoop of ice cream (about 1½ ounces or 3 tablespoons) in each glass. Again, top these scoops in each glass with 1 tablespoon caramel sauce and 1 tablespoon of the chocolate/peanut butter sauce. Finally, top each parfait with a third scoop just like the second one (about 1½ ounces or 3 tablespoons). Top each parfait with 2 tablespoons of the chocolate/peanut butter sauce. Dot each with about 2 tablespoons of whipped cream, then sprinkle 1½ teaspoons peanuts, and serve at once.

Customize It!

Substitute strawberry ice cream topping for the caramel sauce.

Substitute any flavor of purchased ice cream, such as butter pecan, chocolate, maple, or vanilla chocolate swirl, or substitute your own Peanut Butter Ice Cream (page 208) for the vanilla ice cream.

PEANUT BUTTER PUDDING

The deep taste of caramelized sugar blends with peanut butter to make this the richest, smoothest pudding imaginable. As you "burn" the sugar, don't let it get too brown—there's a fine line between caramelized and bitter.

MAKES 6 SERVINGS

¾ cup sugar

2½ cups milk, preferably low-fat or nonfat

1 large egg plus 1 large egg yolk, at room temperature

½ cup creamy standard peanut butter

2 tablespoons cornstarch

1 tablespoon vanilla extract

½ teaspoon salt, optional

1. Place ½ cup sugar in a heavy, medium saucepan and set the pan over medium heat. Cook, stirring, until the sugar dissolves completely, then cook without stirring until the sugar begins to turn light brown, about 4 minutes, maybe more on a humid day.

2. Whisking all the while, slowly but deliberately pour the milk into the pan—the sugar mixture will roil up to the top of the pan and it can burn you, so keep stirring all the while to keep the boiling foam to a minimum. Continue cooking until the sugar again dissolves in the milk. Reduce the heat to very low and keep the milk mixture warm.

3. Whisk the egg, egg yolk, and the remaining ¼ cup sugar in a large bowl until creamy and pale yellow, about 2 minutes. Whisk in the peanut butter and cornstarch until smooth.

4. Pour about half the hot milk mixture into the egg mixture, whisking all the while. Once the combined mixture is smooth, whisk it back into the hot milk mixture. Whisk in the vanilla and salt, if using. Reduce the heat to very low—if you're using an electric stove, use a second burner just now set on low—and continue to cook just until thickened, about 1 minute, whisking all the while. Strain this mixture through a fine-mesh sieve into 6 custard cups and serve in about 15 minutes. Or cool them completely to room temperature, cover with plastic wrap, and store them in the refrigerator for up to 3 days.

NOTES: *To make a richer pudding, fold 1 cup heavy cream, beaten until soft peaks form, into the pudding before you spoon it into the custard cups.*

To avoid pudding skin, place a piece of plastic wrap right down on the hot custard the moment it goes into the custard cups. Refrigerate, then pull off this plastic wrap before you serve the pudding.

Peanut Butter Chocolate Pudding Melt 2 ounces unsweetened chocolate in a small bowl either placed in the top half of a double boiler set over about 1 inch of simmering water or in a small bowl placed in the microwave and heated on high, stirring after every 15-second increment. In either case, once half the chocolate has melted, continue stirring away from the heat or out of the oven until all the chocolate has melted. Cool for 5 minutes, then stir the melted chocolate into the pudding mixture right after you whisk the combined mixture back into the pan with the remaining hot milk.

PEANUT BUTTER SEMIFREDDO

A semifreddo is a classic Italian dessert that's like a partly frozen, marshmallowy ice cream concoction, some fantastic cross between gelato and a frozen pudding cake. (And if you fall in love with this semifreddo, check out the full complement of them in *The Ultimate Frozen Dessert Book*.) Plan on serving small slices of this rich delight in a little pool of chocolate sauce.

MAKES ONE 9 × 5-INCH LOAF PAN OF SEMIFREDDO (ABOUT 16 SERVINGS)

2½ cups sugar

¾ cup water

½ teaspoon cream of tartar

6 large egg whites, at room temperature

¼ teaspoon salt, optional

2 cups creamy standard peanut butter

1 tablespoon vanilla extract

1 cup heavy cream

1. Line a 9 × 5 × 3-inch loaf pan with plastic wrap so that the wrap hangs far over the edges (and will later be able to cover the semifreddo in the pan). Place this lined pan on the floor of your freezer while you make the semifreddo.

2. Stir the sugar, water, and cream of tartar in a medium saucepan set over medium heat until the sugar dissolves. Clip a candy thermometer to the inside of the pan (don't let it touch the bottom) and continue cooking, stirring occasionally, until the temperature reaches 234°F (often marked as "soft-ball stage" on the thermometer—see page 25 for high-altitude candy-making tips).

3. While the sugar is coming up to the required temperature, place the egg whites and salt, if using, in a large bowl and beat with an electric mixer at high speed until doubled in bulk and soft peaks form in the egg whites at the place where the mixer's turned-off blades are lifted out of it.

4. When the sugar syrup reaches 234°F, remove the pan from the heat and slowly beat this very hot syrup into the egg whites, beating all the while at medium speed but adding the sugar syrup in a thin, slow drizzle. Once all the sugar syrup has been added, continue beating until the egg white mixture glistens and the bowl is warm but no longer hot to the touch, about 5 minutes.

5. Beat in the peanut butter and vanilla. Crank the speed up to high and continue beating until the bowl is room temperature, about 10 more minutes.

6. Remove and clean the beaters. In a second bowl, preferably a well-chilled bowl, beat the cream at medium-high speed until soft peaks form.

7. Use a rubber spatula to fold the beaten cream into the peanut butter mixture. Spoon this mixture into the prepared pan in the freezer. Freeze for 1 hour, then fold the plastic wrap over the top of the pan to seal the semifreddo away from any freezer odors. Freeze at least 8 hours or overnight.

8. To serve, peel back the plastic wrap and wipe the outside of the container with warm, damp paper towels to loosen the semifreddo somewhat. Turn the pan upside down onto a serving platter and tap it a few times to get the semifreddo to come free. Remove the pan; peel off the plastic wrap. Serve at once, cutting slices of the semifreddo with a sharp knife and placing them on individual plates.

Customize It!

Fold ¾ cup of any of the following or any combination of the following into the whipped cream before folding it into the semifreddo mixture: butterscotch chips, chopped pecans, chopped skinned hazelnuts, chopped walnuts, Heath Bits, M&M Baking Bits, mini chocolate chips, peanut butter chips, Reese's Pieces, semisweet chocolate chips, shaved bittersweet chocolate, sweetened shredded coconut, or white chocolate chips.

PEANUT BUTTER SOUFFLÉ

Peanut butter gives a traditional soufflé a slightly denser texture, a little cakier and so better able to stand up to lots of chocolate sauce—or as we prefer, a jelly sauce (recipe follows).

MAKES ONE 1½-QUART SOUFFLÉ (ABOUT 6 SERVINGS)

2 large eggs, separated, plus 2 additional egg whites, at room temperature

½ cup sugar, plus additional for dusting the soufflé dish

2 tablespoons unsalted butter, plus additional for greasing the soufflé dish

2 tablespoons all-purpose flour

1 cup milk, preferably low-fat or nonfat

½ cup plus 2 tablespoons creamy standard peanut butter

1 tablespoon vanilla extract

1. Position the rack in the center of the oven and preheat the oven to 425°F. Lightly butter and sugar a 1½-quart, high-sided, round soufflé dish; set aside.

2. Place 4 egg whites in a large bowl and beat them with an electric mixer at high speed until soft, droopy peaks can be made on the beaters when you turn them off and lift them out of the mixture. Set aside.

3. Clean and dry the beaters. In a medium bowl, beat the 2 egg yolks and sugar at medium speed until thick and pale yellow, until it will make satiny ribbons that do not instantly dissolve back into the mixture when the beaters are turned off and lifted up, about 3 minutes. Set aside.

4. Melt the butter in a large saucepan over medium heat, then whisk in the flour. Cook just until bubbling, about 1 minute, whisking all the while. Do not brown. Whisk in the milk in a slow, steady stream; then continue cooking over medium heat, whisking all the while, until the mixture thickens somewhat, about 2 minutes.

5. Whisk about half this hot milk mixture into the egg yolk mixture, then whisk this combined mixture back into the pan with the remaining milk mixture. Reduce the heat to very low and continue cooking, whisking constantly, until the mixture thickens and coats the back of a wooden spoon, about 2 minutes. Remove from the heat and strain through a fine-mesh sieve into a large bowl to remove any bits of egg yolk that have inadvertently scrambled. Whisk in the peanut butter and vanilla until smooth.

6. Use a rubber spatula to fold about half the beaten egg whites into this peanut butter mixture. Very gently fold in the remaining beaten egg whites, using even long strokes with the spatula to keep the egg whites from deflating. There should still be a few threads of white running through the mixture. Pour it into the prepared soufflé dish.

7. Bake for 10 minutes, then reduce the oven temperature to 400°F and continue baking until puffed and golden brown, about 20 minutes. Serve at once.

AN EASY GRAPE JELLY SAUCE

MAKES A LITTLE LESS THAN ½ CUP

½ cup grape jelly
2 tablespoons water

Place the jelly and water in a small saucepan and set it over low heat. Cook, stirring constantly, until the jelly melts and the sauce is smooth. Keep warm, covered, on the back of the stove while the soufflé bakes. Serve by spooning about 1½ tablespoons sauce on each serving of soufflé.

PEANUT BUTTER SWIRL BROWNIES

In *The Ultimate Brownie Book,* we crafted a peanut butter brownie that's far more traditional—a cakier brownie that stands up well in ice cream sundaes. Here, we've crafted a swirl brownie, a light peanut butter and cream cheese swirl in a rich chocolate brownie. Even if you're using a nonstick baking pan, butter and flour it because this small layer will protect the chocolate batter from scorching and turning bitter as it bakes.

MAKES ABOUT 24 BROWNIES

1 cup all-purpose flour, plus additional for the baking pan

½ teaspoon baking soda

½ teaspoon salt

16 tablespoons (2 sticks) unsalted butter, cut into chunks, plus additional for the baking pan

8 ounces bittersweet or semisweet chocolate, chopped

5 ounces unsweetened chocolate, chopped

8 ounces cream cheese, softened to room temperature (do not use nonfat cream cheese)

½ cup creamy standard peanut butter

2 cups sugar

4 large eggs plus 3 large egg yolks, at room temperature

4 teaspoons vanilla extract

1. Position the rack in the center of the oven and preheat the oven to 350°F. Butter and flour a 9 × 13-inch baking pan; set aside. Whisk the flour, baking soda, and salt in a small bowl until the baking soda and salt is evenly distributed; set aside.

2. Place the butter and both kinds of chocolate in the top half of a double boiler set over about 1 inch of simmering water. If you don't have a double boiler, place these ingredients in a medium bowl that will fit snugly over a medium saucepan with about the same amount of simmering water. Reduce the heat so the water simmers slowly, watch out for any escaping steam that can burn your fingers, and stir until half the butter and about half the chocolate has melted. Remove the top half of the double boiler or the bowl from the heat and continue stirring away from the heat until all the chocolate has melted and the mixture is smooth. Transfer the chocolate mixture to a large bowl and cool for 5 minutes.

3. Meanwhile, beat the cream cheese and peanut butter in a second large bowl until smooth, using an electric mixer at medium speed. Beat in ½ cup plus 2 tablespoons of the sugar until smooth, about 2 minutes, scraping down the sides of the bowl as necessary. Beat in 2 egg yolks and 2 teaspoons vanilla until silky and light. Set aside.

4. Clean and dry the beaters. Then beat the remaining sugar (that is, 1 cup, plus 6 tablespoons) into the chocolate mixture using the mixer at medium speed. Continue beating until very smooth and silky, about 2 minutes. Beat in the 4 whole eggs, one at a time, then beat in the remaining egg yolk and the remaining 2 teaspoons vanilla. Turn off the beaters, add the flour mixture, and beat at a very low speed just until the flour is incorporated.

5. Pour three-quarters of the chocolate mixture into the prepared pan. Gently spoon the cream cheese batter over the chocolate one in the pan, taking care to cover as much of the chocolate as you can by gently spreading the cream cheese batter with a clean rubber spatula. Dot the remaining chocolate batter in 1-tablespoon increments on top of the white batter. Use a flatware knife to swirl the two batters together, sticking the knife straight down into the batters and then dragging it in curlicues around the pan.

6. Bake until a toothpick inserted into the chocolate part of the brownies comes out with a few moist crumbs attached, about 50 minutes. Cool in the pan on a wire rack until room temperature, about 1 hour. Using a knife that's safe for nonstick bakeware, cut the brownies into 24 squares and serve. Or store the cut brownies in a plastic container between sheets of wax paper for up to 4 days.

Customize It!

Substitute 2 teaspoons of one of the following flavorings for the 2 teaspoons vanilla extract in the chocolate batter: banana extract, coconut extract, maple extract, or rum extract.

Stir ⅔ cup of any of the following into the flour mixture just before you add it to the chocolate batter: chopped Heath bars, chopped pecans, chopped walnuts, cocoa nibs, dried cherries, dried cranberries, or white chocolate chips.

PEANUT BUTTER TIRAMISÙ

The name of this dessert literally means "carry me up"—some think it implies "to heaven"—because it's traditionally served as an afternoon perk-up. No wonder, what with all the sugar and coffee in it.

MAKES ONE 9 × 5-INCH LOAF PAN (ABOUT 8 SERVINGS)

3 large egg yolks, at room temperature

⅔ cup sugar

5 tablespoons all-purpose flour

⅔ cup creamy standard peanut butter

1½ cups milk, preferably low-fat or nonfat

1 tablespoon vanilla extract

1 cup heavy cream, beaten in a medium bowl until stiff peaks form

About 30 purchased ladyfinger cookies

¼ cup brewed espresso or strong brewed coffee, cooled and mixed with
    1 tablespoon sugar in a small bowl

1. Whisk the egg yolks and sugar in a large bowl until thick and pale yellow, about 2 minutes. Whisk in the flour, then the peanut butter until smooth. Set aside.

2. Heat the milk in a medium saucepan set over medium heat until small bubbles appear along the pan's inner rim.

3. Whisk about half this hot milk into the egg yolk mixture, then whisk this combined mixture back into the pan with the hot milk until smooth. Whisk in the vanilla and set aside to cool for 10 minutes. Fold in the whipped cream.

4. Line the sides of a 9 × 5 × 3-inch loaf pan with ladyfinger cookies, then line the bottom of the pan with the cookies, breaking them to fit as necessary. Sprinkle about half the sweetened espresso over the cookies on the bottom of the pan.

Spoon half the peanut butter cream into the pan over the cookies on the bottom. Lay another batch of ladyfingers over this cream, then sprinkle these cookies with the remaining sweetened espresso. Spoon and spread the remaining peanut butter cream over these cookies. Finally, place a layer of ladyfingers over the top, pressing down very gently to get them to adhere and to compress the dessert just a little.

5. Place the pan in the refrigerator to chill at least 3 hours. Serve at once, or wrap it tightly in plastic wrap and store it in the refrigerator for up to 4 days, spooning out and serving the tiramisù at will.

Customize It!

Slice 2 ripe bananas; lay half the slices on top of the bottom layer of ladyfingers, then the other half on top of the middle layer in the pan.

Divide ½ cup mini chocolate chips between the bottom and middle layers of ladyfingers in the pan.

Omit the sugar with the espresso; instead, stir 2 tablespoons purchased chocolate syrup into the espresso.

PEANUT BUTTER TORTE

This is a kind of American take on a Viennese dessert. You make three layers of peanut-infused meringue (that is, three layers of peanut dacquoise) and then you use a peanut butter cream to fill between them, turning the whole thing into a crunchy, creamy dessert. It's best if it ripens in the refrigerator overnight, so plan on making it a day in advance.

MAKES ONE 4-LAYER TORTE (ABOUT 10 SERVINGS)

6 large egg whites, at room temperature

1 cup roasted unsalted peanuts

¾ cup sugar

1 tablespoon cornstarch

8 ounces cream cheese, softened to room temperature

1 cup creamy standard peanut butter

½ cup heavy cream

1 cup confectioners' sugar, plus additional for the topping

1. Place the egg whites in a large bowl and beat them with an electric mixer at high speed until doubled in volume, soft, and fluffy, about 2 minutes. Set aside.

2. Place the peanuts, sugar, and cornstarch in a food processor fitted with the chopping blade; process until finely ground, about like cornmeal. Gently fold this mixture into the beaten egg whites with a rubber spatula, taking care not to deflate the egg whites.

3. Position the racks in the top and bottom thirds of the oven; preheat the oven to 350°F. Cover two large baking sheets with parchment paper. Use an 8-inch pie plate or cake pan to trace two 8-inch circles with a pencil on each of the two sheets of parchment paper. Alternatively, cut a length of string or twine 8 inches long; hold one end down in the parchment paper and put a pencil at the other end, then use the string to draw 8-inch-diameter circles on one end of the parchment paper, then make another circle on this sheet of parchment paper and two more on the other one.

4. Put a quarter of the peanut meringue in each of the four circles and gently smooth with an offset spatula to fill the circles drawn, thereby creating four circular layers of meringue. Don't press down and deflate the meringue. You can also put the peanut meringue in a pastry bag fitted with a ½-inch tip; begin at the center of each circle and squeeze out the meringue in a spiral to fill in the circle with a coil.

5. Bake until golden and firm to the touch, about 30 minutes. Switch the baking sheets around at least once during the baking to assure even heat distribution. Cool the dacquoise layers on the sheets for 10 minutes, then run a long spatula under them to release them from the parchment paper. Transfer them gently to a wire rack to cool and dry completely, about 1 hour.

6. To make the cream filling, beat the cream cheese, peanut butter, and heavy cream in a large bowl with an electric mixer at medium speed until creamy and smooth, about 2 minutes. Beat in 1 cup confectioners' sugar in ¼-cup increments; continue beating about 1 minute, until a smooth, rich filling forms.

7. Assemble the torte by placing one of the peanut layers on a cake plate or stand. Spoon and spread about ⅓ of the cream filling over this layer, taking care to even out any bumps in the meringue and make a flat, smooth layer of cream. Top with a second dacquoise layer, then spoon and spread about ½ the remaining cream filling on top of this layer as you did with the first layer. Lay a third layer on the cake and top with the remaining cream filling. Finally, top with the last meringue layer. The torte can be stored in the refrigerator for up to 3 days—cover it loosely with plastic wrap to protect it from any refrigerator odors. Right before serving, sprinkle the top layer with additional confectioners' sugar.

Customize It!

Fold any of the following into the filling before you use it between the layers of the torte: ¾ cup semisweet chocolate chips or mini chocolate chips, ⅔ cup Reese's Pieces, ⅔ cup chopped Heath bars, or 1 ounce semisweet or bittersweet chocolate, shaved.

PEANUT PIE

Think of this as a peanut version of classic pecan pie. It's rich, sweet, and a little salty—and even has a peanut butter crust. A slice just begs for a scoop of vanilla ice cream.

MAKES ONE 9-INCH PIE (ABOUT 8 SERVINGS)

FOR THE PEANUT BUTTER CRUST

2 cups all-purpose flour, plus additional for dusting

⅓ cup solid vegetable shortening

½ cup creamy standard peanut butter

½ teaspoon apple cider vinegar

5 to 7 tablespoons very cold water

FOR THE FILLING

4 large eggs, at room temperature

1¼ cups dark corn syrup

½ cup sugar

6 tablespoons milk (regular, low-fat, or nonfat)

½ cup creamy standard peanut butter

1 tablespoon vanilla extract

1 cup chopped roasted unsalted peanuts

1. Position the rack in the center of the oven and preheat the oven to 350°F.

2. Make the peanut butter crust by placing the flour in a large bowl. Use a pastry cutter or two forks to cut and press the shortening into the flour until the mixture resembles coarse meal. Then cut in the peanut butter until the mixture has a coarse, sandy texture. Add the vinegar, then 5 tablespoons of the water. Use a fork to mix until a mass begins to adhere, adding more cold water as needed to yield a fairly moist but not sticky pastry dough.

3. Sprinkle a few drops of water on your work surface, then lay a large piece of wax paper onto the work surface. Dust the wax paper with flour, then place the dough in the center. Dust the dough and a rolling pin with flour, then roll out the dough to a 12-inch circle, dusting with more flour if the dough starts to stick to the rolling pin. Pick up the wax paper with the rolled-out crust on it and invert it into a 10-inch pie plate. Position the circle so that it fits perfectly into the plate, then peel off the wax paper, gently pressing the dough into place in the pie plate. Trim the edges, or crimp them into a fluted pattern, or use a fork to make decorative marks around the edge of the crust. Set aside.

4. Whisk the eggs in a large bowl until lightly beaten, then whisk in the dark corn syrup, sugar, and milk until smooth. Whisk in the peanut butter and vanilla, then stir in the peanuts. Pour this mixture into the prepared crust.

5. Bake until the filling sets when the pie is gently shaken, about 50 minutes. If the fluted edges of the pie begin to brown too darkly, you can cover them lightly with thin strips of aluminum foil to prevent their scorching. Cool the pie on a wire rack for at least 1 hour before serving. Once completely cool, the pie can be stored in the refrigerator, covered tightly in plastic wrap, for up to 4 days.

SOURCE GUIDE

Online Suppliers

www.birchboy.com
Fantastic, exotic syrups from Haines, Alaska, including elderberry, highbush cranberry, spruce tip, and our favorite, birch.

www.boyajianinc.com
A wide range of flavored oils and vinegars. Many of their products are available at high-end markets, but the entire collection is available online.

www.importfood.com
A complete online store of Thai products, including curry pastes and rice noodles.

www.kitchenkrafts.com
A complete line of candy-making and baking supplies.

www.quickspice.com
A huge online resource for Asian ingredients and equipment.

www.pacificrim-gourmet.com
A full range of Asian ingredients and kitchenware.

Brick-and-Mortar Stores That Will Ship Products

Broadway Pan Handler
www.broadwaypanhandler.com
477 Broome Street
New York, NY 10013
866-COOKWARE or 212-966-3434
One-stop shopping for bakeware, cookware, knives, and more.

Kalustyans
www.kalustyans.com
123 Lexington Avenue
New York, NY 10016
800-352-3451 or 212-685-3451
The place for international one-stop shopping for East Indian products, including nut oils, exotic flours, flavorings, and dried fruits.

Kam Man Food Products
www.kammanfood.com
200 Canal Street
New York, NY 10013
212-571-0330
One of New York's finest Asian grocery and cookware stores with a comprehensive line of Asian oils, vinegars, sauces, and dried noodles.

Kitchen Market
www.kitchenmarket.com
218 Eighth Avenue
New York, NY 10011
888-468-4433 or 212-243-4433
A great source for Latin American and Mexican foods, including chiles and spices.

Marshall's Honey Farm at the Flying Bee Ranch
www.MarhallsHoney.com
159 Lombard Road
American Canyon, CA 94503
800-624-4637
Great honey of all varieties from apiaries in northern California.

New York Cake and Baking Distributors
www.nycake.com
56 West 22nd Street
New York, NY 10010
800-942-2539 or 212-675-CAKE
Every baking and candy-making necessity imaginable.

Penzeys
www.penzeys.com
800-741-7787
Tons of stores across the Midwest and South with a huge online catalog for spices and some of the best vanilla extract available.

The Wok Shop
www.wokshop.com
718 Grant Avenue
San Francisco, CA 94108
888-780-7171
In the heart of San Francisco's Chinatown, a store with a huge assortment of woks, rice steamers, bamboo steamers, cleavers, sushi mats, and other Asian cooking equipment. Nearly everything is also available online.

Uwajimaya
www.uwajimaya.com
600 5th Ave South
Seattle, WA 98104
206-624-6248
An enormous Asian grocery store with three retail outlets in Washington state and Oregon.

www.ultimatecook.com
At our ultimatecook website, you'll find extra recipes and information on all the *Ultimate* books, as well as our schedule, tips, reviews, and other fun information.

INDEX

waffles, peanut butter, 49–50
White Russian, frozen peanut butter, 132

yeast breads:
    honey oat, for ultimate PB&J, 16–20
    peanut butter, 64–66
    peanut butter coffee cake ring, 29–31
    peanut butter sticky buns, 43–46

    ultimate white, for PB&J marshmallow cream
      sandwich, 21–25
yogurt:
    in peanut butter biscuits, 27–28
    in peanut butter gingerbread, 59–60
    in peanut butter lhassi, 138
    in peanut butter smoothie, 140
    in peanut lamb curry, 108–9